Woman *of* Steel

Woman *of* Steel

VIVIEN CHERRY
WITH KEITH WHEATLEY

Adlard Coles Nautical
London

in association with

Coopers
&Lybrand

Published 1993 by Adlard Coles Nautical
an imprint of A & C Black (Publishers) Ltd
35 Bedford Row, London WC1R 4JH

First edition 1993

ISBN 0–7136–3795–1

A CIP catalogue record for this book is available from the British Library.

Typeset in 12/14 Baskerville by Selwood Systems, Midsomer Norton, Avon
Printed and bound in Great Britain by
Butler & Tanner Ltd, Frome and London

CONTENTS

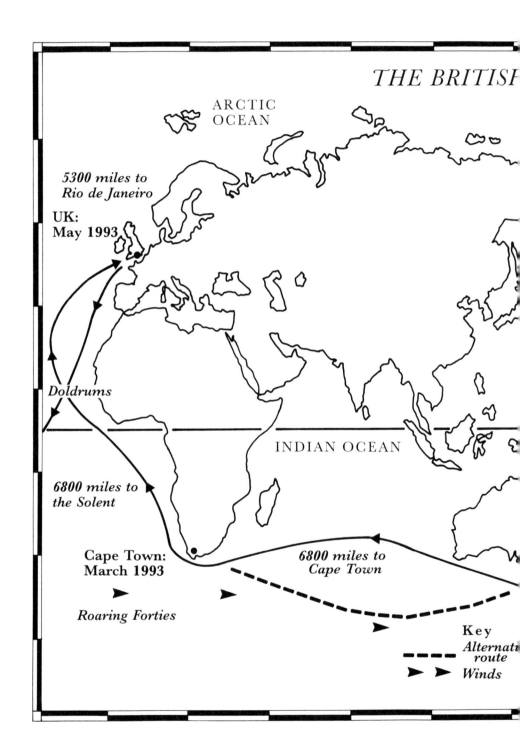

ARCTIC
OCEAN

*5300 miles to
Rio de Janeiro*

UK:
May **1993**

Doldrums

INDIAN OCEAN

*6800 miles to
the Solent*

**Cape Town:
March 1993**

▶

Roaring Forties

*6800 miles to
Cape Town*

▶

Key
*Alternati
route*
▶ ▶ *Winds*

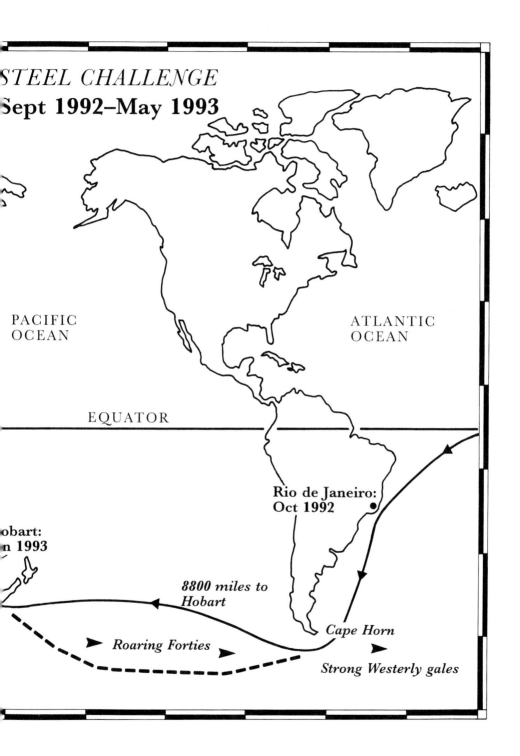

STEEL CHALLENGE
Sept 1992–May 1993

PACIFIC
OCEAN

ATLANTIC
OCEAN

EQUATOR

Rio de Janeiro:
Oct 1992

obart:
n 1993

8800 miles to
Hobart

Cape Horn

Roaring Forties

Strong Westerly gales

Preface and acknowledgements

This is my personal account of life on *Coopers & Lybrand* during the British Steel Challenge, pieced together by Keith Wheatley from journal entries and observations during the course of the race. The speed with which the book was put together and the agonising that Keith must have been through to extract my thoughts and emotions is a credit to his journalistic ability.

I have tried to give not only an account of the race itself, but also an insight into my feelings – my frustrations, insecurities and my particular blend of lack of tact mixed with decisiveness, sympathy and understanding which combined to produce a circumnavigator. As this is my personal view, those of my fellow crew will probably differ drastically, even though we all spent the best and worst part of eight months together on the same boat somewhere on the oceans of the world.

It was truly an exceptional challenge and the adventure of a lifetime – one which I am very proud to have been part of. I would like to express my great thanks to Chay Blyth for allowing me to take part in his dream. My thanks also go to the members of the Challenge team and all in the Race Office; to my family and friends for their support and patience in listening to my endless Challenge problems; to Coopers & Lybrand UK and their international offices for their efficient organisation and support around the world.

Finally, a very special thanks to my crew for all their hard work and their support through the good times and the bad times, and I sincerely wish them luck with all their future ventures.

Vivien Cherry
June 1993

Illustration acknowledgements

The author and publisher would like to thank the following for permission to reproduce photographs on pages 69 to 72 and 105 to 108.

Mark Pepper/Kodak/Nikon/PPL
  Page 72 (bottom left)

Neil Skinner/Kodak/Nikon/PPL
  Pages 69, 70 (bottom), 71 (top), 72 (top and bottom right), 105, 106 (bottom), 107 (top), 108

Coopers & Lybrand/Kodak/Nikon/PPL
  Pages 70 (top left and right), 71 (bottom), 106 (top), 107 (bottom)

The drawings in Appendix 1 were provided courtesy of Thanos Condylis of C & S Yacht Designs

Edward Scott of BT for his assistance in selecting the plots of yacht tracks reproduced on pages 50, 89, 116 and 173.

Foreword

Those of us who have long relished the excitement
and the rigours of yachting will understand and
perhaps even feel a twinge of envy on reading of the
joys and the deprivations experienced by the crews of
the British Steel Challenge yachts as they cir-
cumnavigated the globe. As patron of the Challenge
and president of its official charity, The Save the
Children Fund, I followed their progress with great
interest from the start.

What impressed everyone associated with this bold
adventure is the degree of dedication and sacrifice
which imbued the 140 volunteer crew members: all
are amateurs and many had never before sailed when
accepted by Chay Blyth to participate in the race.

I feel certain that all the competitors will in some
way have found their lives to have been changed as a
result of the opportunity to take part in this unique
endeavour and hopefully their achievements will serve
as an inspiration to others to rise to similar challenges
in the future.

HRH The Princess Royal

Pre-race:

January 1989–
September 1992

CHAPTER 1

Meet the Challenge

The shrill cry of 'man overboard' pierced the roaring tumult of the storm with heart-stopping clarity. I felt the bile rising in my throat in an instant fear reaction. For a split second everything stopped, then I hit the man overboard button on the GPS, giving a precise location. Matt dashed to take off the brake on the propeller shaft so that the engine would be ready for immediate use. We found Brian over the side, at the limit of his harness, with his forearm clamped around a stanchion. He had been on deck replacing the heater exhaust caps and the first thing he said was, 'I didn't lose the caps, Vivien. Here they are, keep them safe, I didn't lose them.' He handed them up to me before we hauled him back on board. A crisis averted – but one which uncovered our darkest fear about this, the toughest yacht race ever undertaken; if another of us was swept from the deck into the mountainous seas in the Southern Ocean, would we be as lucky as Brian?

My course towards the British Steel Challenge had really begun almost five years ago. Breaking through into the big league of offshore sailing is never easy for a young skipper, male or female but opportunity knocked for me in 1988 with the Observer Singlehanded Transatlantic Race. I had the chance to borrow the excellent *Panicker*, a 40 foot fractional-rigged sloop which was specifically designed for single or twohanded racing; this proved an offer I couldn't refuse.

One pays a high price for competing in these fascinating, self-absorbed events. I knew that I would probably have to sell my flat to pay for the campaign and change jobs, too, in order to find the time to do the race, but it was something that I really felt compelled to do. I was very nervous – I would be competing against people who had done these races before; there were major French heroes such as Florence Arthaud and Phillipe Poupon, plus British legends such as Chay Blyth to contend with. *Panicker* and I suffered rather a slow start out of Plymouth Sound but then we really got in the groove and the boat began going superbly well.

From the very first night I had a problem with the autohelm and it continued to plague me for the first three or four days. During that early stage of the race I had no sleep and was hand-steering virtually all the time; if I wasn't actually on the helm, I was working at sail changes. Then we had a bit of a blow from the north giving huge seas and really black nights. At that point I had, I suppose, the worst experience in my sailing life. I was over-tired – absolutely whacked. I was hallucinating and, almost certainly, driving the boat around in circles.

Panicker was knocked flat twice. The second time did the trick; it drenched me and woke me up. I went forward and took the headsail off, tied it all down and said to myself, 'I've got to trust the autohelm now – I need sleep.' I slumped on the berth below, still wet through, and fell asleep. In actual fact I was totally oblivious for four and a half hours. I awoke stiff and sore, but the boat was still there and I was still in it. I was amazed to find that the boat was also going in the right direction. We had travelled 28 miles whilst I was dead to the world, which wouldn't have been a bad average even if I had been on the helm; so I put the kettle on and resolved to have a little more trust in Fate.

Curiously, this story came back to me in the very early days of the Challenge when I first met my crew at the Earls Court Boat Show. I had felt it was important to show that first of all I didn't know everything, secondly one could cope with things going wrong, and thirdly one would get through it. This story of the knockdown, the hallucinations and the boiling kettle on the Observer Singlehanded Race was the one I used to try to introduce myself to them.

The earliest days of my involvement with the Challenge were in September 1990. Jock Wishart, an old friend and sailing companion, had been having dinner with Chay Blyth at the Southampton Boat Show and had discussed Chay's forthcoming British Steel Challenge. Following the huge publicity received by the *Maiden* crew in the Whitbread Round the World Race, which had finished four months earlier, it was clearly a good concept in media terms for the Challenge to have at least one female skipper. Chay was enthusiastic about the idea of having a woman skipper. Although the Challenge had received dozens of enquiries from women wanting to take part in the race itself, of the 20 or so applications from skippers at that time, only one had been female – and she lived on the other side of the world. Jock knew my capabilities and felt confident enough to suggest me.

'Do you still want to go sailing to make your living?' he coaxed. 'If you do, I've got Chay Blyth's phone number here and I think you should give him a call.' I didn't actually know Chay Blyth but we had twice before taken part in the same races – the 1985 Round Britain Race and the 1988 Singlehanded Transatlantic. Of course, Chay was a generation older than me, a national hero and the 'grand old man' of British competitive sailing. I was female and comparatively inexperienced, and here was Jock urging me to pick up the telephone and say 'Hello Chay, you don't know me but I'd like to skipper one of your yachts in the Round the World Race.'

It took me a good three or four days to pluck up the courage to make that call. When I did ring, it was Chay himself who answered. He was his usual dry Scots self and suggested, with no great enthusiasm, that I should drop him a line. The resumé of my sailing life and career went more or less as follows.

My first contact with sailing was in my father's Mirror dinghy back in 1968. He had always had a hankering for boats and decided to build a sailing dinghy in the garage. We were living at Kinloss in northern Scotland at the time, as Dad was stationed there as an RAF pilot. I was eight and my brother Robert was nine when we first put the dinghy on top of the car with a caravan behind and set off for a tour around the Scottish coast.

The Mirror dinghy was a great success – you could pile in all the family plus the dog and go off for a picnic. One incident which I clearly remember from that first trip was my brother, wearing his lifejacket, starting to row the dinghy away from the jetty on his own. He leant back as he pulled on the oars then let go – and the oars went floating away. Seeing this, I dived in off the quay to swim after the oars. I can still remember that nasty shock of very, very cold water which took my breath away.

Family circumstances and house-moving left the Mirror lying neglected for a year or two. It wasn't until I was 14 and we were living in Sussex that I thought about the dinghy again. It was a hot, boring summer and I persuaded Dad to take the Mirror down from the roof of the garage and go sailing at Shoreham. It quickly became apparent that we had outgrown this old friend, so the family bought a Wayfarer. At this stage, horses were the great passion of my life – I would even babysit for people for the chance of riding their horses. Boats were Dad's hobby but we would go along and join in when we had spare time or when we felt like it, usually sailing from Bosham near Chichester.

I eventually went to University at Loughborough, which is about as far from the sea as you could possibly get in Britain. However, I joined the university sailing club and sailed Fireflies. While I was at university, my father had a little windfall and decided to invest in a small cruiser, a little South Coast One Design. Sailing with families can be fraught, as anyone who has done much of it can testify. But all through my university years and despite our conflicting schedules (my father was still working as a pilot) we managed to sail together quite often on the SCOD. My brother was away doing VSO in Tanzania so I became my father's main sailing companion, a press-ganged crew. In some ways it was an unlikely combination, but we needed each other in order to go sailing and learnt to rub along and form a team.

The week after I finished my finals, Dad gave me a very influential present. He booked me on a Day Skipper course at the national sailing centre in Cowes. The course started on a Saturday and it blew a gale all week. There were three of us on the course: one chap who had some dinghy experience, another who had just bought a trailer sailer, myself and the instructor. Despite the weather we had a marvellous time and I loved it. I found that I had an aptitude for bigger boats and was fascinated by the skills which were needed to sail them, such as the ability to sail the boat up to a mooring and stop it in the right place at the right time. I found that I desperately wanted to develop those skills and 'get it right'.

The summer of 1981, when I graduated, provided an example

of the way my working life and sailing life would be hopelessly intertwined from now onwards. I'd found myself a job in London and a flat to move into. The weekend before I was to start the job was the Cowes to Poole SCOD race, which I was keen to take part in. However, my father was away and it was going to be the first time that I'd skippered and taken charge of a boat on my own. Somehow, everything came together at the same weekend. We completed the race, which I'm sure we would have won if I had only been able to find the finish buoy! We sailed back from Poole on Sunday, arriving back to the Chichester mooring late in the evening. I rushed to pack a suitcase, find my work gear and a kettle and left for London sometime after midnight to begin my career as a Building Services Engineer.

After that SCOD race I never looked back. We spent three years racing the family boat, *Peter Baker*, all along the south coast and took her across the Channel several times to France. I joined the London Corinthian Sailing Club because it was just down the road from my office, and I managed to spend the winters falling into the freezing Thames at Hammersmith out of an International 14. Once I was part of that serious racing crowd the invitations to race on bigger, faster boats began to arise. I competed in the initial Royal Ocean Racing Club (RORC) race of the season on *Cabadah*, a Sigma 33, and other races on Sigmas too.

Unbeknown to me, the owner of *Cabadah*, Gordon Greenfield, was to play a supporting role in this British Steel Challenge. He and Chay Blyth went back together a long way, and once I had applied for a skipper's job Gordon gave me great support in terms of reassuring Chay that, as I hadn't sunk his boat thus far, I would probably be safe with one of Chay's. The other big development for me was the chance to take part in the 1985 Round Britain Twohanded Race. A friend, Peter Hopps, was planning to enter in a 40 foot trimaran. His original crew could no longer make it and he asked me if I was up to the campaign. It was way beyond anything I had tackled before in sailing terms, but it seemed enormously exciting, so why not? By the time we left Lerwick, half-way round the course, we had just about learnt to sail the boat. Sailing a race campaign by the seat of my pants was not entirely novel, but nothing had prepared me for the scale of the challenge to come.

The Challenge itself was a curious 'dream on a plate' – a

£15,000 sail around the world package, in effect. It attracted people who were more interested in finding out about themselves than being racing sailors. If I expected more than that then, with hindsight, my analysis was faulty. Because I am obsessed with sailing for sailing's sake, I had wrongly expected that most of the crew would share my feelings. The process of finding out about each other's expectations would be an intriguing and traumatic process which was to continue all the way round the world.

These were my original crew of volunteers:

Brian Bird, 51. Brian, a butcher, discovered sailing five years ago. He paints for a hobby and every canvas has a boat hidden somewhere. His wife, Hazel, is a teacher. Brian is strong, both mentally and physically and was to prove a real asset as a crew member. He has both the RYA Competent Crew and Day Skipper certificates and is a qualified scuba diver.

Paul Titchener, 29. Paul, an accountant with Coopers & Lybrand, has sailed in dinghies since the age of nine. He was the most experienced sailor among the volunteers and the natural choice as mate.

Samantha Wood, 23. Sam has a degree in philosophy which, she says, makes her less employable than anyone else on the boat. On a passage crewing from St Lucia in the West Indies, she loved the sailing, hated the calms – but then looked for ways to sail more. Her aim was to come back with the confidence to do anything in the world that she wished to do. Sam proved to be an easy-going and reliable crew member.

David Turner, 33. David became hooked on sailing by reading *Swallows and Amazons* and is now following his dream. He works as a financial adviser with pensions and was given a ten month leave of absence. He planned to go back to work after the Challenge but will reconsider life as it comes. He has a strong character and is a natural organiser; he is always concerned for the wellbeing of others.

Neil Skinner, 34. Neil uses work as a means to an end: summer jobs on the road or trucking, with three or four months travelling, produce the money to spend during the winter. He has been to Nepal, India and Israel and usually ends up living with friends.

His aim was to take on more responsibility and stick with a job for a longer term. Prior to the Challenge he had completed several transatlantic yacht delivery trips and so had good experience to offer.

Gary Hopkins, 35, worked for the Central Electricity Generating Board until he changed careers and became a building surveyor. He sailed at school and then bought his own dinghy. Gary went on to race Hunter 27s and won at Burnham week in 1991. Although he missed much of the initial training, his sailing experience was useful.

Matthew Steel-Jessop, 29, is a computer network manager – fit enough to run a marathon, but a complete novice when it came to sailing. Matt's real aim was to prove to himself that he could complete the arduous day to day, week after week hard work and concentration of the Challenge. The Challenge training had shown Matt to be a fast learner and an excellent sailor and organiser.

Richard Griffith, 49. Richard is a company director and a high flyer in the world of aircraft sales. He is a very determined man who, as soon as he became involved with the Challenge, gained useful experience by delivering a yacht to the Caribbean.

John Kirk, 49. A blunt ex-paratrooper, who had always been involved in physical activities, John was reserve for the 1968 Olympics team as a middle distance runner. He then became an instructor at an outdoor activities centre. I hoped that his stamina would inspire the rest of the crew when the going got tough.

Robert Faulds, 29. A printer who has his own yacht, Robert was one of our more experienced crew. He expressed an interest in the catering side of things and the foredeck.

Murray Findley, 61. President of his own linen company in Las Vegas, Murray made a point of flying over for the Boat Show, determined to meet his fellow crew. His next visit to England was for the delivery trip to London and the naming ceremony. He proved to be a keen and dedicated sailor, popular amongst the crew.

Jill Ireland, 30, originally trained as a veterinary nurse but became interested in sailing when working for the John Lewis

Partnership. She has endless drive, enthusiasm and a bubbly character. She tended to doubt her own ability to complete the Challenge.

There were four people due to join us for one or more legs. They were:

Ann de Boer, 26. A PR executive who once worked for Jock Wishart and was also involved in the early days of the Challenge through working on her company's Nuclear Electric account. She had no previous sailing experience.

Phillip Jones, 28. Phillip was a British Steel employee from the Port Talbot steel works. He had a good deal of sailing experience in small keel boats: Ospreys and J24s.

Michael Bass, 28. Another British Steel employee, this time an electrician from the Teesside Division, Mike had no previous sailing experience.

Paul Shepherd, 40, is a fitter in a stainless steel works in Sheffield. He is a marathon runner but with no sailing experience.

Not long after the Boat Show, I invited the crew round to my boyfriend Tony's house in Ealing, where I was living. I wanted to try to engender some feeling for one another without the crowds, spotlights and the general hubbub of the Earls Court Show. I had certain plans for that day – I wanted to set the groundwork of how the boat was going to be run. I intended to outline my first thoughts and let the crew think about them. I wanted them to see that their skipper was organised, had a brain and used it; I intended it to be a well-run boat.

I asked each volunteer to introduce themselves in a five minute chat, as I was interested to find out why they wanted to do the Challenge and what they thought they were going to get out of it. I outlined how, on a boat, everyone needs to have a specific job or area of responsibility. From this meeting plus the information that they had given to me in letters and responses on a questionnaire, I had a first stab at allocating people to jobs and specialist areas. I was aiming at a high level of competence from individuals in two areas, and the ability to act as back up in a third area.

Most of us were quite young. We had four people aged around the fifty mark, the rest being in their late twenties or early thirties, but none in early middle age to balance the group. We consisted either of people whose families had grown up and left home or single people who weren't married and didn't have a family. I was aware that we were all physically fairly small; I don't think, at that time, it worried the others. There was a buzz of excitement as the project started to come together. The crew now knew who their skipper was and they knew that their sponsor was the international accountancy firm, Coopers & Lybrand. I thought I had got off to a reasonable start, but I was still very anxious to make a good impression so they would follow me.

At the beginning, the crew were happy to have me as their skipper. After that good start, things went fairly rapidly downhill; for a lot of different reasons I suppose. I think my nervous reaction to the responsibility of it all came through as I felt my way through a job that I hadn't done before, having to teach myself as I went along. Communication at team level was difficult – crew members would get offended if I shouted at them on the boat and take it very personally. So, although I had made a good initial impression, we still needed to get to know one another. That was going to take a few painful months yet – painful on their side as well as mine. Almost the only thing we all had in common was an avid keenness to do this voyage. Everyone seemed to have completely different reasons and motivations, but at this stage we all had 100 per cent dedication to the project.

In mid-March, nearly three months after the Earls Court encounter, I decided it was about time that at least some of the crew and I actually got on to the water together. We had done a lot of talking, writing and telephoning about how we were going to go round the world, but the strange fact was that we hadn't got as far as sailing a boat. We chartered a Sigma 38 – which cost me a fortune – from Lymington for a weekend and set off. It was blowing force 8, which was useful for a crew who were planning to sail round Cape Horn but it didn't provide a wonderful starting point for the weekend.

Still, it counted as a successful weekend – we started and finished with six live crew, the mast was still upright and there wasn't too much shouting – not counting mine, which was allowed. After the first weekend it was apparent that everyone on board, with the exception of myself, was more keen to get to know one another and chatting about their lives than on working and racing the boat. It was obvious to me that my main concern was going to be to try to overcome this and put training into effect that would help them concentrate and become racing sailors.

The notion of training presented its own confusions and mis-understandings. Our crews were presented to the skippers as 'trained'. Certainly, during the preceding two years, they had spent several sessions aboard the original prototype yacht based in Plymouth, but there was only one yacht available for the 130 trainees. Furthermore, in the months immediately prior to the crew's arrival in Brixham, it had been exhibited on the British stand at Expo '92 in southern Spain and so was unavailable for training.

To an experienced racing sailor, my crew looked keen but with a great deal still to learn. One classic example, in the early days, was the way in which they would grind a winch, looking at the winch all the time rather than the sail that they were trying to trim. In the six months from joining *Coopers and Lybrand* in Brixham to departure, I still only had the crew aboard for a maximum of four to five days a month, so continuous training was out of the question and there was insufficient time even to get to know them as individuals. Little wonder we lacked cohesion as a team when our 28,000 mile odyssey began for real.

CHAPTER 2

Steel Hulls and Iron Skippers

Beyond the fact that Chay had begun talking of the race as 'the toughest yacht race ever' and that it was, in some sense, a re-creation of his own round the world solo voyage 21 years earlier, I had no detailed knowledge of what I was getting into. It seemed a good idea to do a little research into Chay and his background – after all I had been a mere child in my dad's home-made Mirror dinghy when Chay had been sailing around the world in the first *British Steel*.

This pugnacious little Scots ex-paratrooper first became a house-hold name when he set himself the task of rowing across the Atlantic in 1966 with Captain John Ridgeway, also of the parachute regiment. Although specially designed for the voyage, it was still just a small open boat and the British newspapers had a field day with it. When the voyage ended, Ridgeway and Blyth featured on magazine covers from *Stern* in Germany to *Newsweek* in the United States. Chay made the almost unbelievable statement that it was his first trip in a boat, although since then he has sailed in every conceivable floating object. For him it was simply another exercise in survival – the kind of thing he had been doing in the Radfern Mountains above Aden with three parachute regiments. But it opened extraordinary new doors for this tough little soldier from the border town of Hawick in the south of Scotland.

I went to the local library and borrowed a copy of Chay's book about his solo voyage around the world in 1970–71. One extract from Christmas 1970 particularly impressed me; it read: 'My Christmas present from the Southern Ocean was a disaster – a huge sea hit the yacht and smashed the self-steering gear beyond repair. I was hurled across the cockpit, my head hit the companionway and my forehead was gashed open. It was a deep nasty cut. I was more concerned about the self-steering gear though; with that out of action the whole voyage had to be seen in a different light.'

It made me realise, with quite a jolt, that this was not only going to be a personally testing voyage, but one with considerable potential for harm and even fatal risk to the people I was taking with me. I began to look at the whole aspect of the volunteers who were coming to take part in the race and wonder what was motivating them.

When Chay announced that he was going to stage this Round the World Race and was going to be asking ordinary people with little or no experience of sailing to pay nearly £15,000 and give up nine months of their lives for the opportunity to live in extreme discomfort, cold and even danger, most of the pundits both inside and outside sailing told him he was mad. Yet that first week when the race was announced at the London Boat Show still lives on in Challenge folklore.

There were 164 applicants for the 10 skipper posts, following press advertisements and media coverage and the initial briefing was at the Earls Court Boat Show in January 1991. A shortlist was drawn up, resulting in 45 interviews followed by the selection of 22 people who were invited to sail on *British Steel Challenge*. These 'trials' were slotted in as part of the Challenge tour around Britain at the end of June. My introductory trip was from Southampton up to Bristol. Then followed a nerve-wracking time as we waited to hear who had been selected. The reality of my successful application came with an invitation to dinner at the RORC on the evening prior to the public announcement of the 10 Challenge skippers in November 1991.

Curiosity about the identities of the skippers was uppermost in my mind as I walked into the bar. I found that I already knew two of them: Pete Goss and Mike Golding, whom I had sailed against in the 1988 Singlehanded Race; I had also heard of John Chittenden, the master mariner and Whitbread skipper. The others had a great deal of sailing experience and their careers were closely linked with yachting. The final line up of the other nine yachts and skippers were:

Interspray Paul Jeffes (39) is a naval architect and the managing director of a boatyard, Silvers Marine in Dunbartonshire; he has accumulated some 20 years sailing experience.

Rhone-Poulenc Alec Honey (49)*, like Chay an ex-paratrooper, had run a sailing school in France and had been a watch leader on Chay's *GBII* Whitbread boat. Although not professionally connected to yachting at present, he has a sound sailing pedigree.

Pride of Teesside Ian MacGillivray (36) is a professional yacht skipper from Southampton. He has a boat building background and has also been a sailing instructor; he assisted with the training of Challenge volunteers.

Hofbrau Lager Pete Goss (31) is an ex-Royal Marine who has been awarded various trophies for outstanding seamanship. Pete earned my respect by racing a small catamaran *Cornish Meadow* across the Atlantic, when I wouldn't have ventured outside Plymouth harbour in it! He was the Challenge Training Manager.

Group 4 Securitas Mike Golding (32) was another competitor in the 1988 Singlehanded Race. He is a keen multihull sailor and Ocean Yachtmaster instructor. I felt a certain kinship with Mike as he is, like myself, an amateur sailor; he works as a fireman. His past experiences of capsizes with his trimaran gave him a keen knowledge and awareness of survival and safety techniques.

British Steel II Richard Tudor (33) has his own sail making business in Pwllheli, North Wales. He has an extensive racing background and is a member of the Pwllheli lifeboat team.

Commercial Union Will Sutherland (45) followed a career of teaching outdoor activities before specialising in management training using sailing as the training medium – an ideal background for crew training.

Heath Insured Adrian Donovan (34) is an ex-Merchant Navy officer who became a sailing instructor and charter yacht skipper. I remember being stung by his introductory assumption that, because I was a woman, I was one of the Challenge secretaries!

Nuclear Electric John Chittenden (52) is a master mariner with a wry

* Unfortunately Alec Honey had to resign before the race started as his wife had fallen ill. He was replaced by John O'Driscoll (49), a Lieutenant Commander given leave of absence from the Royal Navy and with some 42,000 miles of racing and cruising experience.

sense of humour and a long seafaring family background. He skippered *Creighton's Naturally* in the 1989 Whitbread Round the World Race and was the only Challenge skipper to have sailed round the world.

Soon after my selection as a skipper, I began to hear stories of how people had simply stopped what they were doing when the race was announced, whether it was the ironing or a piece of work on their desk, and headed towards London to sign their name on an entry form and a cheque, in order to change their lives. Richard Griffith, one of my future crew saw the television announcement of the Race and, on impulse, decided he wanted to sail round the world. In some ways it resembled a mini medieval crusade. I was at that Boat Show myself, with friends from the London Corinthian Sailing Club, and I knew about the project. Several of my friends were eager to sign up although none did. I was more reluctant, partly due to a natural meanness and unwillingness to part with the necessary initial £75, but also from a knowledge that this voyage was something that I very much wanted to do – yet I also knew that I had the experience and capability to do this at some point in the future on my own terms.

Part of me wondered whether I was going to fit very comfortably into the ethos that Chay was creating, much though I admired it. As events unfolded, that was to be a percipient warning voice. I did, however, identify with one very strong aspect of the British Steel Challenge. My own background was not one of privilege, of gin and tonics on the yacht club verandah watching Daddy's yacht come in. Chay, an extraordinary man from a very ordinary background, had a goal which was to inspire millions of other ordinary people to go and see what he had seen and do what he had done. He gave a newspaper interview around that time which impressed me deeply. 'Thousands, maybe millions of people want to sail, but don't because it is seen as elitist,' he said. 'It's not – although the first time I went to a yacht club I felt really uncomfortable. In those days I could barely string three words together. Sailing is a risk sport and full of excitement and adrenalin, but it is nowhere near as dangerous as rugby or hunting. If you don't want risk or excitement buy a bag of cotton wool and sit inside. No-one is compelling anyone to go on this race.'

As an engineer I was interested, naturally enough, in Chay's decision to build the race yachts out of steel. For equivalent size and displacement they would be far heavier than boats built of GRP or some exotic composite, as for instance modern top class racing and Whitbread yachts are. But when you have a fleet of identical yachts – One Designs as they are known in the yachting business – racing together and against one another, such considerations become meaningless. Indeed the extra weight became a positive virtue in the heavy seas that the crew encountered along the 28,000 mile route with much of the sailing to windward. A certain amount of extra displacement actually makes a yacht *easier* to sail to windward. It tracks better and thrashes against the helm less wildly than a lightweight boat will.

A ductile material like steel would fare better than a more rigid material of the same technical breaking strength. It also has the virtues of durability and fixability. Very often the crew of, say, a Whitbread yacht will include people who have actually undertaken the specialised task of building the composite hull. I knew that none of my collection of butchers, bakers and candlestick makers were going to be boat builders, and it was certainly a relief to know that the yacht was going to be constructed of a material that, hopefully, would never need patching together by the crew.

Another reason for choosing steel had been that the yachts were to be built at the somewhat unlikely venue of Devonport Management Limited, better known in its previous incarnation as the Royal Navy Dockyard in Plymouth. While this venerable institution had been hitherto more familiar with putting guns on frigates, steel does lend itself to mass production of boats, and this proved to be an area where the dockyard skills were superb. As soon as I went aboard the first yacht, I was struck by the excellence of the technical construction, the standard of the welding and the quality of the fit out below decks.

Like the Sigma 33, which I raced with my father, the Challenge yachts were designed by David Thomas. The number of Sigmas taking to the water each weekend and their extraordinarily good safety record and after-sale value shows that Thomas does know what he is talking about when it comes to building durable racing yachts, and it was certainly a plus point to know that he was the designer. He had repeatedly asserted that the considerations of strength and safety were paramount in his mind when designing these boats, and for me, as a skipper who was going to be responsible for the well-being of the crew living aboard for extended periods, that was a comforting initial thought to have. David Thomas' particular skill was in his ability to create yachts in which it was relatively easy for the crews to sail well; and with practice and talent, achieve the optimum speed potential of the boat.

Any combination of hull and rig will have an optimum speed potential. The crucial test is how easy it is for the crew to reach that optimum. The easier it is the closer the racing will be. This is what happens weekend after weekend in the huge Sigma fleets which regularly race around the coast of Britain. More and more competitors are attracted to the class every year. Success now becomes a question of tactical planning and crew skills in keeping the yacht as close to its optimum speed as much as possible. Of course, the skills of mastbend and sail twist remain relevant, but on these boats they are achievable by people without massive levels of experience; so the challenge for a skipper like myself was going to be to keep people attentive, motivated and concentrating. I wasn't going to need a team of experts to sail *Coopers*; just people who were keen to learn, would concentrate 100 per cent and become expert in their area to enable the team to race this yacht.

David Thomas predicted that the British Steel Challenge would see whole groups of yachts finishing within minutes of one another after thousands of miles of racing. Certainly anyone who saw the fleet sail into Rio after the first leg from Southampton will have realised how true that prediction was to be. The 10 sloops, 67 feet in length, each carried a cutter rig which divided the 1932 sq ft of sail into 3 separate components – a mainsail and two headsails: the yankee and staysail. The philosophy of this was to make the sail plan both more manageable and more easily repairable for long distance sailing – although that's hard to believe when seeing the No. 1 yankee filling the space below decks on a rough day. We also carried a No. 1 genoa which we used for lighter airs.

Down below, the yachts were very well appointed. There were 14 bunks, one for each person on board, divided into 6 cabins. In the bow were a pair of 'heads', port and starboard; next to these were the 2 berth cabins with long bunks, then came the smaller, slightly cramped 3 berth cabins. The central doghouse area comprised the chart table and three seats suitable for wet sailors. This nerve centre and pivotal point of the yacht was busy with crew moving either out on deck or through the yacht to their cabins while others got dressed in or undressed from foul weather gear. The choreography required at watch changes became known as the 'Doghouse Shuffle' and the 'Foulie Locker Fall' – a common result of bad footwork.

Further aft, down three steps, were the galley and saloon areas. Although not quite large enough to seat 14 people in comfort, it was ideal for large gatherings of up to 10 crew. Right at the stern were the last 4 berths, one of which was mine – the port-side coffin bunk.

I had already reflected, when first meeting my crew, on how physically small we seemed against the task facing us. It was a tribute to the well thought out philosophy behind the Challenge, that by dividing the sail plan into smaller and more manageable units, the sails themselves would become smaller and that crews which were physically less strong would not be disadvantaged. In this race it was going to be brain power rather than brawn that counted. If there was a disadvantage with a yacht as heavy and as solidly built as this, a Rolls Royce of a racing yacht if you like, it was that when training relatively new sailors, the boat was necessarily slow to respond. It was never going to be sensitive and give a good feel when, for instance, trying to teach sail trim in the earliest days. There was a tendency for a novice helmsman to oversteer making sail trim more difficult; it was hard to convince him that a certain technique would produce extra speed when initially there seemed very little apparent difference.

When I had the chance to take some of the crew sailing on my father's much lighter and faster Sigma they were absolutely astonished at the way the boat quickly responded to changes in helm and sail trim. Of course, one cannot have the best of both worlds, and very few people would contemplate paying £15,000 to race around the world the wrong way in a Sigma.

The other surprising thing for me about the yacht's specifications was the enormous power of the communications network, as well as the usual SSB radio and radar. Each yacht was to be fully equipped with the Inmarsat C system. This gives data communication 24 hours a day with race headquarters via telex. What I had no means of guessing at this early stage was the sheer volume of communications that was going to pour into the boat. It was partly due to the publicity that the race created and the response engendered in friends and relatives of the crew. Also there were the demands of the sponsor who, having invested heavily in the yacht's participation in the race, wanted to keep firmly in touch with their prodigy. Naturally, too, the media had become aware of the race's appeal to the general public and began to make ever increasing demands for news. So the telexes and requests began to pour in.

Not so long ago, a yacht at sea or even in harbour was one of the most peaceful places on earth. People went sailing to escape from the office – now it seemed that the office was in pursuit. Meshed into this system was an **IBM** laptop which was used primarily for the reception and production of weather pictures. The reports would be fired off to race headquarters back in Hampshire once a day via Inmarsat C. The volume of information from each yacht, both numerical and narrative, meant inevitably, I suppose, that the role of skipper became somewhat akin to living in a goldfish bowl; this was certainly true in the months before the start of the race.

Although I had been a racing sailor for some ten years or more, I was by no means experienced in the ways of the world when it came to sponsorship of international sport. Although £15,000 per person seemed like a lot of money, Chay had realised in the earliest days of the Challenge that it was going to be necessary to raise at least £225,000 in sponsorship for each yacht from commercial companies. Sailing is one of the areas of sport where sponsorship has grown incredibly fast in the past ten years. The traditional image of blue blazers and white ensigns has firmly moved aside to accommodate the companies and corporations that are willing to pay for this exhilarating sport which also costs a great deal of money at the highest level. Chay Blyth had done an extraordinary job, in conditions where the recession was rapidly becoming a reality, to persuade corporations as diverse as Nuclear Electric, Hall and Woodhouse, Group 4 Securitas and Coopers & Lybrand, the international accountancy partnership who were to sponsor my yacht, to become involved in such an ambitious and, as yet, untried scheme.

Although the fee paid by each of the sponsors to participate was identical, what became rapidly apparent was that their degree of enthusiasm, commitment and willingness to spend more cash on everything from crew uniforms to corporate hospitality would vary enormously. It was a curious situation that was bound to cause anomalies. The crews and skippers had not chosen their sponsor, nor had the sponsor chosen that skipper or crew in the way that, say, they fully expected to choose their own employees. Were we working for ourselves, for, Chay, for the sponsor, or a mixture of all three? It was a question that was bound to arise and it certainly did over the months leading up to the start of the race and many times thereafter. Each group had their own legitimate expectations from what was, potentially, a volatile mixture.

Inevitably there were occasions when the interests of each group simply seemed to contradict those of the others. The piggy-in-the-middle was always going to be the skipper, as I rapidly discovered. If Chay had been to any degree cynical in deciding, after the huge publicity success of the *Maiden* crew in the Whitbread race, that he needed a woman skipper as part of his programme, I had no feeling that I was merely a token female skipper. I was sure I was qualified for the job, and he was prepared to offer it to me, so why should I bother about the commercial or other motivations that lay behind it? Although I had seen the response towards Tracy Edwards and her *Maiden* crew by the public during the progress of the previous year's Whitbread race, and had even been aware of the 50,000 people who turned up to see the pink yacht return home safely up Southampton Water, I don't think I was truly prepared for the level of media interest I was to generate as the only female skipper.

As far as handling media attention was concerned, after a brief presentation and some scant notes we were left very much on our own by Chay and Challenge. They had other concerns, and simply didn't have the resources to get involved in every small request for a newspaper or radio interview. The consequence was that, as a newly-retired engineer rather than an experienced PR person, I was left to handle this tricky area myself with the help of Jessica Mann, the public relations manager at Coopers & Lybrand. At times the request for interviews became a deluge and I was aware that I was not handling all of them as well as I should have done. However, although the Challenge may not always have had the time to help out in these areas (a lot of this was left up to the individual sponsors), they were inevitably extremely sensitive to the consequences. Chay was always inclined to be fairly dismissive of newspapers, referring to them as 'fish and chip wrappers'. His view was that any printed word or comment in the press was very shortlived in people's memories. Yet for someone who wasn't bothered by the press he had an uncanny knack of knowing almost every line that had been in print anywhere in the country about the Challenge. It increased my feeling of living inside a goldfish bowl.

There was no practical method of preparing our crews, and ourselves, for the physical and psychological experiences of sustained bad weather at sea. The Challenge had done its best to provide suitable training during the previous two years. Pete Goss, the training skipper, had worked non-stop to take all the volunteers out on the prototype yacht. From an initial familiarisation sail, they progressed to heavy weather sailing before the final placements. Pete had virtually spent the whole of one winter beating *British Steel Challenge* around the Eddystone Light on a short course off Plymouth. Nearly every 20 minutes, the volunteers had to undertake some manoeuvre, course or sail change. From the stories which the crew told me, this was designed to weed out the weak volunteers but the actual outcome was to strengthen their resolve to continue.

The skippers would try to explain to their inexperienced crews how horrendously cold, wet and uncomfortable it would all be; even the simplest of jobs, like taking in a reef, would take a very long time. It would be dark with the boat bucking round madly and the tail end of the sheet (or line) would be whipped out of freezing fingers. Crew would struggle to complete tasks whilst their bodies were continually being bruised and battered. It sounds nasty enough and it does bring a bit of a chill to the spine, but in the end they are only words. Our training race around the Fastnet Rock did in the end provide some rough nasty weather, but only for a relatively short space of time. Perhaps as trainers we were worrying about the impossible. There is simply no way of reproducing the conditions and psychological problems of weeks at sea in a relatively small boat in a challenging and deeply hostile environment.

That summer, between collecting the boats at Easter from Brixham marina and the final race start on that glorious Saturday down the Solent was, in all probability, the most stressful part of the entire Challenge. So much was being learned for the first time. So many people with so many agendas – many of them incompatible with one another. As the publicity bubble and 'hype' became bigger and bigger, it sometimes became hard to see where reality was in all of this. I don't think it's an unfair criticism to say that, at this point, the Challenge business – the commercial vehicle Chay had created to run the race – was significantly under-resourced for the task it faced. Chay had achieved a minor miracle in taking his concept from a dream to the reality of ten fully-equipped ocean-going yachts sitting in the marina at Ocean Village in Southampton, each with a crew and a skipper. Some of the differences and the inevitably incompatible roles assigned to people would produce a situation that would come to a head months later in Rio de Janeiro.

The individuals aboard each boat were both clients and crew. Of course, the skipper was in charge, but these people were the paying customers; without them there would be no race and no job for the skippers. Unlike any other race I had either heard about or taken part in, the skippers themselves were paid employees of the Challenge business. Our contracts included guidelines on when we could talk to the press and what about. To borrow a phrase from another sport, Chay was running a game where he had the bat, the ball and owned the pitch, yet the idea of total control was somewhat illusory. The great majority of the people signing up for the race had themselves been successful in their own professional lives. They were used to taking charge, making decisions and making things happen their way – in other words, achievers in their own right. The ones that didn't have this background at least had the confidence that comes from having written a very large cheque and buying their share of what they wanted.

Although each skipper possessed the theoretical sanction of refusing to sail with a crew member whom he or she thought might endanger the safety of the yacht, it was an extreme measure and one not to be used except in the most dire circumstances. The reality was that we were all stuck with one another and would have to make it work. Occasionally a serious policy difference that might have been resolved, had there been more time for discussion, was inevitably just papered over in the frantic rush of that summer. Like a juggernaut with a mind of its own, the Challenge developed its own momentum – its own track through the water. We were clinging on to the deck and trying to influence its course in small ways. But in reality Chay was the man at the helm, once more going solo with the rest of us hanging on behind. It's hard to see how it could have been any different. No large well-structured organisation would ever have had the originality to come up with something as exciting as the British Steel Challenge. It was bound to be the brainchild of one extraordinary individual. That was both its strength and possibly its weakness.

Chay gave one characteristically bullish interview where he said 'What I am good at is raising the money and giving the participants and the sponsors what they want. There is nothing new in any of this. After all, Queen Isabella sponsored Columbus'. It was a good quote and justifiably received wide publicity, but at times during those five months from taking delivery of the yacht in April to the start in September, I felt as if I had as clear an idea of what lay ahead of me as Columbus must have done when he sailed westwards aboard the *Santa Maria* in 1492.

CHAPTER 3

Building a Team

I officially became skipper of the 40 ton yacht *Coopers & Lybrand* at Brixham, Devon on the inauspicious date of 1 April 1992. My parents took me down to the little fishing port to collect the boat. It was at the moment that we drove over the hill and I saw the line of ten white masts that I finally believed the Challenge was a reality and that the race was going to happen.

Coming from a building background I knew that any major project has a tendency to run late and be over-budget yet, with a slight sense of disbelief, I saw that there were the boats, completed on time, all ten of them, and they floated.

I was immediately struck by what marvellous colour schemes each of the ten individual sponsors had conceived for their yachts. They looked so striking sitting there in the small harbour. Perhaps we have all become so used to the traditional muted whites and blues of production yachts that to see imaginatively and expensively painted hulls in corporate colours can be an enormous and pleasant shock. I thought at the time, and still think that my own sponsor, Coopers & Lybrand, had designed one of the prettiest colour schemes, with the stripes making the boat look longer and thinner.

It was comforting, in a relatively strange environment, to meet the other nine skippers but we were like new trainees arriving at our first job. Although we were obviously to become rivals at a later stage, at this point we all had a great deal more in common than we had separating us. We had all met briefly before at a Challenge weekend, although most of the group were strangers to me apart from Pete Goss and Mike Golding who had been in the 1988 Singlehanded Race. It was fascinating to see the Challenge technical director, Andrew Roberts, behaving very much like a protective mother with his babies. He had lived with this project for nearly four years and here were the gleaming new yachts – proof of his endeavour and technical expertise. We, the new skippers were acting like owners who had come to take away his treasured charges. If he was reluctant to hand them over, he was gracious enough not to make it too difficult; we couldn't wait to get our hands on them.

The first big anticlimax for me was four nights aboard without sleep. There always seems to be a slight swell in Brixham marina and the skipper's aft cabin is right on the curb of the counter stern. The little waves would slap under the stern right beneath my head with the whole steel hull reverberating like an oil drum. After four nights I had slept in, or at least tried to sleep in, at least half the bunks on board the empty yacht. With the help of a few Brixham beers and the wearing off of the initial excitement, I finally got some sleep.

A yacht this size is a fairly complex piece of engineering and we skippers had to spend the next ten days making sure that we knew how things worked and where the various plumbing and cabling runs were. Whatever we learned at this point about the internal construction and fit-out of these boats, was certainly going to stand us in good stead in the event of a mechanical breakdown or something similar off Cape Horn.

One thing I definitely wasn't looking forward to was actually slipping the lines and taking *Coopers & Lybrand* off the quay. Although I had sailed thousands and thousands of miles, many of them on my own, I had very little experience of manoeuvring a yacht of this size and weight in a confined space under power. In fact I had no experience at all. After ten days it couldn't be postponed any longer. A ceremony was due to take place and we had to move the boats all of one hundred yards to the events pontoon. Luckily there was no wind, and I persuaded Andrew Roberts to come with me as a comfort factor. I started the 120 horsepower Ford Mermaid engine, cast off the lines and nosed *Coopers & Lybrand* out on her short first voyage with me at the helm. Nothing went wrong, but it was definitely as nerve-wracking as anything that was to come later on the voyage around the world.

The period between then and Easter, the middle weekend of April, was one of intense activity and preparation. Although the yachts were technically finished, they were far from stored and equipped. They needed everything from halyards to gas bottles; bunks had to be fitted and tools stowed. Many of the crew came down to help during this commissioning period. It was very much a party type atmosphere around the Brixham marina. It was the first time that the crew volunteers had met or gathered en masse with the yachts and had the chance to meet members other than the ones from their own yacht. It was like the first night back at school after the holidays.

At Brixham I think we first realised that when it came to victualling the boat we would be better off relying on our own resources than on the Challenge organisation. The logistics of ordering food for 10 boats and 140 people were very taxing for the Challenge Purchasing Officer, Alistair Hackett. When the food arrived for the voyage up to Southampton we found we had a huge number of tins of fruit. I began to wonder what Alistair generally lived on when he went sailing. Anyway it took us a good five months before we had eaten our way through the fruit that was embarked at Brixham.

We left Brixham on Easter Day 1992. It wasn't to be a race up to Southampton; our only instructions were to be there to rendezvous with the other yachts for a photographic session at midday. Unfortunately, everyone's expectations of a sparkling sail up Channel were disappointed as there was little breeze, so we motored steadily east leaving Berry Head behind us. I had appointed two of the crew as navigators for the passage up to the Solent. It proved to be an early indication of how much of a one-man band I would have to be in the early days. I had overestimated their level of training, interest and expectation of the whole trip. It illustrated the fundamental misconception I had made about the nature of the people taking on the task. Because they were making a financial sacrifice and a big personal effort to go on the voyage, I had instinctively tended to think of them as people who would initiate things – that is to say they would be proactive rather than reactive. The keenness was certainly there, but it needed very detailed application and direction, and I should have realised I needed to give more of that. Whatever the different perceptions, the end result after two hours hard labour over the chart table was a passage planning detail that would have scarcely enabled me to motor around Torbay. Classic errors had been made, such as changing charts but not checking the scale, so that on the new chart one mile was measured off as five miles. However, with further time spent, the passage plan was knocked into shape.

It was an uneventful passage. The only irony was that having agreed to rendezvous for a photo opportunity one mile south of the Needles, we found ourselves in thick fog and rendezvousing effectively by radar rather than by eye. However, fate smiled on us that day, for although it was foggy beyond Hurst Castle and the Narrows, it was brilliant sunshine in the Solent itself. The fleet emerged from the west out of the fog to permit a sequence of fleet pictures off Yarmouth. After a fairly tense session of close quarters manoeuvring for the benefit of a photographer and a helicopter with forty tons of yacht and a crew who were still very much learning the ropes, the last thing I needed or expected to see was an inflatable dinghy with an outboard buzzing around us. Only after swearing vociferously at the driver to get out of the way did I realise that it was my boyfriend Tony. He had obviously been sailing with some friends, was in Yarmouth for lunch and had decided to pop out and see us.

The photographic schedule called for us to have our spinnaker hoisted. It was the first time *Coopers & Lybrand* had sported the monster sail, and it would be fair to say that relatively few of us on board had a clear idea of what was going to happen when it was hoisted to the masthead. Somehow it went up and down in one piece and the photographer was happy and we were ecstatic! On deck there was a sense of considerable achievement.

The next stop was Ocean Village, the marina on the southern edge of Southampton's former dockland; this was to be our new home for the remainder of the summer. The Challenge office was set up here and the ten yachts berthed in a reserved area of the marina.

There was an unexpected bonus for myself, the crew and the sponsor in late April on the day of the fleet baptism. Princess Anne was due to name *Pride of Teesside* which was the tenth and final yacht to find a sponsor; unfortunately *Teesside* developed a technical problem which meant she couldn't go out that day. A call came over the VHF to ask for the next yacht to contact Andrew Roberts. It was us, and pretty soon we were alongside the pontoon embarking HRH and her entourage. It was a foul wet day to take anyone sailing, let alone a royal guest. We bashed down Southampton

Water into the wind and rain, sailed around for a bit and finally stopped in Osborne Bay for lunch. As a sailor herself, and one who had just bought a new boat, Princess Anne was interested and encouraging in everything we were doing. It was a sign of how new *Coopers & Lybrand* still was that black foul sandblasting grit was coming out across the deck. The Princess even joined the rest of the crew with brush and bucket, to sluice away the black dirty mess.

During this first month I was still the only full time member of *Coopers & Lybrand's* crew. I was living aboard in Ocean Village armed with a mobile phone, trying to get everything organised – from corporate sailing days to more training for the crew. It was a hectic time and I began to feel overwhelmed by the numerous and diverse responsibilities and lack of resources to meet them all. The next big trip in *Coopers & Lybrand's* schedule was in early May to a lavish photographic and publicity session at St Catherine's Yacht Haven next to Tower Bridge, London. I had invited my old friend Jonathan Clark, an experienced dinghy sailor and columnist on *Yachts and Yachting* magazine to come on the trip as a guest. I was looking forward to seeing what he made of the Challenge after an opportunity to see it from the inside. Having heard a gale warning, I also felt it would be a confidence boost for me to have him along for the trip.

By the time we were off the Goodwin Sands the wind speed indicator was registering 52 knots across the deck. Ten of the crew were seasick and we had shredded the spinnaker coming up the Channel earlier that afternoon. I think that the brief period between blowing up the kite and being in the gale off the Goodwins when conditions were really unpleasant was a real shock to a lot of the crew. I could see them thinking to themselves 'Shit, this is bad and we are only in the Channel; what's it going to be like in the Southern Ocean?' I responded probably in too blasé a fashion for some of them by saying that I would rather be in a deep ocean in this kind of weather than five miles off the Goodwin Sands where your navigation has to be absolutely spot on because of all the ships and ferries everywhere. Nevertheless it was to prove a considerable eye-opener for most of the crew.

Despite the battering, we arrived in St Catherine's and moored up. Here we met the Coopers & Lybrand sponsor team headed by Rod Perry, for the first time. Rod has a keen interest in sailing and races his brother's Sigma 33. He and his team were full of enthusiasm for the Challenge and they proved to be quite different from my image of accountants. They were responsible for all the support and administration, ranging from the design of the colour schemes on the boat to the handling of the corporate entertainment and interest generated by the sponsorship. We spent the day shining and scrubbing for the sponsor's naming ceremony on Monday. There were bits of extra clothing and extra crew arriving from all directions; it was a frantically busy time.

After our sponsors had given the crew dinner on Monday night I had the first serious inkling that things were going wrong between the crew and myself. Titch and Brian approached me, not because they were the focus of discontent but because they were among the more considerate and understanding of the crew and were possibly my supporters. They told me that things were not right and that a proportion of the crew were deeply unhappy with my leadership. It was a very hard blow. It's a shock, when you think you have been doing your best to drive this rather curious project, to be told that, in fact, rather than being seen as a leader you were being seen as a failure. I really hadn't expected to have to deal with such an emotional, tired and upset crew and when people get like that, particularly in a group, they can become very bitter and very hurtful. It became clear that the root of the problem was that when I felt I was just giving a plain instruction, it was taken as an implication that something was deeply wrong and that it was a criticism of the person concerned. It was surprising, indeed amazing, how emotionally affected some of the crew could become over an instruction concerning a different sail trim or a simple piece of gear handling.

So much of what I was saying was being taken as personal insults that it began to appear to me that there might almost be no useful way of instructing this group. After all, in only twelve weeks or so, I was supposed to be taking them on a voyage around the world – a voyage that Chay Blyth had already told them was going to be 'the toughest yacht race in the world'. It was hard to see how I was going to get there with people who might get upset if advised to trim a genoa sheet slightly differently. In any other job or situation, one might have just walked out. It certainly bruised my confidence and ability to do the job. After Titch and Brian had spoken to me about the mood on the boat, I sat on the stern in St Catherine's dock and wept quietly and wondered how I was going to resolve this question. It certainly wasn't easy to contemplate the four days of training to come and the trip back to Southampton with a crew, split between those who merely disliked me and those who actually wanted me off the boat.

The issue that no-one amongst the crew raised at the time, or indeed later, was the fact that I was a woman skipper, indeed the only woman skipper. Later in the summer one of my fellow skippers, Paul Jeffes from *Interspray*, did make the point to me that people might react badly to exactly the same words or instructions coming from a female skipper, that they would expect and take quite calmly from a man. He wasn't trying to indicate that this was exceptional or rational, just that it was a fact, and indeed it would be how he would react. It made me wonder, subsequently, whether a lot of the hostility was due to exactly this difficulty although it was sublimated and not expressed.

After the London trip we also began to see the first uncertainties in the crew composition. Murray had business worries in the States and good cause to be at home near his business in Las Vegas. But I am sure that the effect of our rather unhappy voyage to London had some influence on his decision to take part only in the first leg. Understandably perhaps, after such an upheaval, the mood on the delivery trip back to Southampton from St Catherine's was subdued and quiet. The confrontation may have helped to clear the air as there seemed to be a willingness to learn and an openness by everyone that had been sadly lacking in the weeks beforehand.

Although it was fundamental to the concept of the Challenge that it would be a One Design race it was also becoming apparent that some boats were more equal than others. Perhaps this was inevitable due to the nature of sponsorship and competing corporations. Some of the companies backing the yachts were willing to throw considerable amounts of time and money into coaching programmes. Jock Wishart managed to organise free help with coaching the crew from local Hamble stalwarts, Jim Saunders, Ian Stowe and Fiona Brown who, between them, managed to instill the basics. *Rhone-Poulenc* had engaged the services of the renowned French single-hander and previous Whitbread winning skipper, Lionel Pean as crew coach. He had been aboard the yacht during the Fastnet training race as a fifteenth person. It was obvious that any yacht would benefit from having a helmsman and tactician of

Pean's experience aboard on a long ocean race, particularly with a crew of relative novices. Once back ashore the skippers as a group were less than thrilled about the ruse, regarding it as 'out of order' but the most vociferous and deeply held feelings were amongst the crews themselves, who virtually exiled their colleagues on *Rhone-Poulenc*. That ugly word 'cheating' was certainly heard in the bars and cafes around Ocean Village.

Coopers & Lybrand helped with a training weekend at Chilworth Manor, near Southampton, at the end of May. Set amongst beautiful surroundings, Chilworth was chosen in part because it had a fitness centre which would supplement the mental training with physical exercises to help us perform as a team.

One of the exercises included dropping an egg from a first story window, having first devised equipment to catch it made from a balloon, elastic bands, paper and sellotape. One of the more entertaining physical exercises consisted of teams of five people in line walking on wooden 'skis' through an obstacle course. Of course, this became a race between the teams; it certainly high-lighted difficulties of working together.

The mental exercises were just as demanding; concentrating on our motivations for doing the race, both individually and together, and asking how we would achieve our objectives. We all had to put into words the chaotic jumble of feelings, aims, strengths, weaknesses felt by all. Our strengths included enthusiasm, stamina, flexibility, and 'liking the wet end'. The qualities we would need included humour, the ability to generate mutual encouragement and comradeship. The conclusion of the weekend focussed on our main aims. We found that we all wanted many and varied things from the Challenge, amongst which were 'to complete the race safely with a sense of achievement', 'to do our best to win' and 'enjoy what we were doing.'

Out of the thirty available days in June, only four were allocated for on board crew training; all the other days were taken up by main sponsor and sub-sponsor events, most of which all the yachts and crews had to attend. At the end of June the Challenge fleet sailed to Holland giving additional training days on board. All ten yachts visited Scheveningen for the christening of *Group 4*, whose sponsor is based there. It was Group 4's opportunity to have the whole fleet in one place for their corporate entertaining and hospitality.

It was on the delivery trip back from Scheveningen that we had our next confrontation aboard the yacht. Richard came to see me and said that there was a slight groundswell of unhappiness aboard the boat and it might be as well to call a meeting to try to get whatever it was out in the open again. After the good training sessions we'd had and an apparent improvement aboard, I was scarcely willing to believe that we had reverted to the awful atmosphere at St Catherine's Dock in May. It was a hot windless day as we motored down the Channel. With hindsight, that might have had something to do with the actual tone of the meeting. Two or three brisk sail changes usually provides enough focus to vent any feelings or surplus emotions.

So we convened on deck for a crew meeting with me as the focal point. I had set myself up ready to be shot down and the arrows certainly were poisoned that day. As an instinctive loner it was possibly a lack of understanding on my part that people needed attention and praise just to get on with what they had already chosen of their own free will to do. Like children, the crew seemed to constantly seek my approval. John Kirk, the ex-paratrooper aboard with a strong military background, insistently asked what training or experience I had in leadership. Although I had run a racing yacht with a crew of seven for three years quite successfully, I had to concede that in the rather confined military terms in which John posed the question, I had no leadership training or background at all. Having previously followed a successful career and raced yachts successfully on my own terms, it was extremely painful to be so heavily criticised.

This confrontation had an emotional effect on me, which may have been exactly what the crew needed to see. If they had been unable to accept me wholeheartedly as the figure of command, they seemed somewhat more willing to accept me as an upset, vulnerable human being. It might not be the conventional role model for a yacht skipper, especially a racing yacht skipper, but on the other hand there was very little that was conventional about this whole situation.

Once back in Southampton, I knew that the only people who could possibly understand this bizarre situation were my fellow skippers but on the whole the experience and the emotions it brought forth were still too raw to discuss with my colleagues and rivals. I had an inkling that Will Sutherland aboard *Commercial*

Union was going through something similar with his crew, but in a way that made me want even less to talk to him about it. I desperately wanted to avoid setting up a mutual moaning session that would become more destructive than constructive. One or two of the other skippers such as John Chittenden and Adrian Donovan occasionally let slip with a kind word or observation that they knew things were tough for me, but I had their confidence and I really wasn't in a mood to acknowledge in public how much internal doubt and worry the crew dissent was causing me. After all, the essence of being the skipper is to be the person in charge. If you start wandering around wringing your hands and asking 'What to do I do next?' you don't exactly inspire confidence either in your peer group or those you are supposed to be leading.

Unlike other demanding jobs, the post of being a Challenge skipper was one you lived 24 hours a day. There was no door you could close and say 'Well that's over with till tomorrow morning!' You were living on the yacht, you were point-man in terms of direct contact and responsibility for the sponsor, for the crew, and for the Challenge itself. Everything passed through the skipper. Chay always backed his skippers to the hilt and made it clear to the crews that they had his full confidence and delegated authority. However, from a personal point of view, if you are feeling vulnerable and a little fragile, someone as physically capable, gung ho and 100 miles an hour as Chay Blyth, is probably the last person on earth you would choose as a confidant for your worries and your fears.

The administration and organisation taxed all the skippers during that very hectic summer. Although, by May, we all had mobile phones and were easily contactable, the task of ringing up each crew member once a week could take up to three hours with no guarantee that I would be able to reach everyone. I had formatted the summer programme into tabular form, listing all the crew's names so, at a glance, I would know who would be sailing and when. This programme and any briefing notes would be updated and sent out by Coopers & Lybrand. This became a regular 'Crew News' which continued for the duration of the race to keep all our families and friends informed.

I felt I was being drawn three ways: to the Challenge, the sponsor and to the crew so I had very little time left to give to my family and friends. I had lists everywhere: equipment, race plans, training, clothing, photographs; even so it was hardly surprising that a few things were left out. We had to become flexible enough to switch from discussing subjects like sail trim to checking the device for breaking the champagne bottle and ensuring that flags would be available for the naming ceremony.

My pet hate became the clothing; the sizes were often wrong, items were missing, the blue trousers were late arriving, and no one liked the white shorts. It became a nightmare which would plague me for the whole race!

In early July came *Coopers & Lybrand's* debut as a racing yacht. The Challenge had set up its own special race from Southampton down to Ushant at the north west corner of France, around the Fastnet Rock and then back to Southampton. It was to be a course of nearly 750 miles and quite a tough test for boat and crew.

It was interesting that at a training weekend, staged not on the sea but inland during May, there had been lengthy discussions about motivations for taking part in the Challenge. Out of the group only a handful listed winning the race as a prime objective. So our first race together was going to be an interesting intimation of who amongst the 14 of us on board was really a racer and who wanted to sail around the world – two quite different things. Matt was certainly amongst the most competitive on board. As a marathon runner, he knew about competition and he knew about the endurance and stamina it takes to win a long distance event. Amongst the others who shared similar attitudes were Neil, Robert, David, Brian and Titch.

However, there was a much more worrying factor aside from the crew's personal motivation. Mutual discontent and disharmony between myself and the crew had been simmering all summer and this had come to a head the day before the race. Probably the crew expected something different from a skipper – maybe something that involved the training, but as we were all strangers, the learning curve of getting to know one another was fairly traumatic and painful. It was an unhappy situation at that time and I discussed it with Chay. He arranged a meeting on board with all the crew and myself, and he explained the basics. He said 'This is your skipper – this is the professional sailor who has certainly my utmost support and respect.'

Although it was a less than perfect way to start a big race, it at least brought to a head some of the discontent that had been rumbling on through the last two months. Chay's technique of having a group meeting and then asking each individual to talk to him privately meant that they had to focus their grumbles and worries in a rather more articulate way than simply saying that 'the skipper was no good' or that 'Vivien had to go'.

For myself, I was glad in a way that the meeting had happened. I knew I wasn't going to quit this job, although it had been extremely difficult and I had no idea when I started how hard it would be to try to weld this group of individuals with different motivations into an ocean-going crew. Chay had told each of the crew that he would speak to them again when they came back from this race to see if their feelings and wishes remained the same. I knew I was going to be on trial to a certain extent as we set off down towards the start line.

It couldn't have been a more frustrating day for a crew that were hyped up and raring to go. It was the lightest of summer days in the Solent. We crossed the start line off Gilkicker Point at 9 am, but it wasn't until 6 pm that evening that the first yacht passed the Needles. It was ironic that this first day of training designed for deep ocean racing was almost entirely influenced by tide. We stayed well offshore of the Channel Islands to dodge the current and it put us at Ushant in fourth place. The mood aboard was buoyant – we were well placed, no-one was seasick, the weather was fine and at last we were doing what we had talked about for such a long time.

Like all solo and singlehanded sailors I had developed the habit of being awake most of the time, sleeping in just two hour snatches and trying to be aware of everything that was happening on board the boat. It may have been natural for me but it wasn't entirely the way my crew would have chosen to run things. Somewhat understandably they suspected that I was around so much because I didn't trust them. It was natural that, when they wanted to take responsibility for longish periods, they would find it unsettling when the skipper reappeared on deck after she had gone below to her cabin only half an hour or so earlier.

Although the weather was relatively moderate, never rising above force 6 or 7, changing headsails at midnight in 30 knots of breeze is still somewhat different from anything that the training weekends had prepared the crew for. Neil in particular, who had made a number of delivery trips as a yachtsman, was convinced that I was pushing the boat too hard for the conditions and indeed that I wasn't safe, and to his credit had no hesitation in voicing the opinion. However, it never became a contentious problem, because the weather quickly deteriorated and half the crew dropped like flies with seasickness. Once again we were seeing the truth of the old adage that there is no training like the real thing.

After 48 hours of racing and watch keeping, despite their previous training, the crew were starting to show signs of tiredness. With the experience later gained on the legs of the real race it was easy to see that we were more in training than racing mode. For instance we were bearing away for headsail changes to keep the foredeck as flat and dry as possible – something we would have laughed at doing months later. As we neared the Rock, still in fourth place, we saw the leaders *Rhone-Poulenc* and *Interspray* bearing down towards us under spinnaker in slightly over 30 knots of breeze. I remember thinking at the time, 'Rather them than me.' I couldn't see that, with our crew in the current modest state of preparation and experience, we were going to be flying any spinnakers at night in that level of wind.

Coming up to the Fastnet Rock we were tack for tack against *Hofbrau* when we encountered a hindrance entirely of our own making. As we tacked I shouted at Ann and Murray to get the mainsheet fully wound in. Ann called back that it was in hard already and that the block was solid. As I called 'Keep winding, keep winding,' she replied just as firmly that she couldn't. What they hadn't noticed was that the bottom hem of Murray's foul weather trousers had been gradually drawn through the mainsheet block, completely jamming the entire mechanism. Once we realised what had happened, I shouted for a sharp knife to cut it free, I could sense a moment's apprehension as to whether it was going to be the trousers or his foot that was sacrificed!

The trip back from the Rock was the downwind run that everyone who sails to the Fastnet hopes for. It was blowing about 30 knots and at first we sailed with a poled out No. 1 yankee until daylight. I went down below for some rest and John, Matt and Titch had the opportunity to feel the helm. It was good practice for them to experience helming downwind with a rolling following sea. Once I had had some sleep, however, we hoisted the spinnaker and I steered for about three hours. It was very hard work. These are very big heavy boats and at first I was reluctant to let some of the other crew members with much less experience take the helm. Not long after I handed over the wheel to John, the seam that was already starting to fail on the spinnaker gave up the ghost completely and ripped from side to side. It was back to poled out headsails for the rest of the race.

We sailed into the Solent in sixth place which, everything considered, I was reasonably happy with. The mood aboard was a vast improvement on the period immediately before the race began. The six days at sea full-bore racing (the first time for most of the crew) had generated a sense of fulfilment. We had managed to complete the race, with no disasters; there had been a few laughs and we had done reasonably well compared with the rest of the fleet.

If July was the month for racing, August was the month of corporate hospitality. Cowes Week was followed by an intensive programme in subsequent weeks. It was the month of chilled white wine, French bread and cheese out on the Solent. We sailed with corporate hospitality guests for seventeen straight days out of eighteen. It was both a pleasure and a strain – a pleasure in the sense that so many of the guests were high achieving, imaginative individuals who had reached senior positions in their companies or organisations and brought great insight and often original observations to what we were hoping to do. It sounds like an endless party, but the reality was: up at 7 am every day, clean and tidy the boat, bring down the food, the wine, the ice – not all the easiest of commodities to transport across a marina – and make sure the crew were in spotless uniforms and with polished smiles to greet the guests. The timetable required us to be back alongside at 4 pm. Even on the days when that was achieved, the whole process then went into reverse: clean up the boat, drink the wine, possibly get ready for an evening function and then up again at 7 am the next day to repeat the whole procedure. If our smiles wore a little thin by the end of August it was probably understandable.

A good deal of the last few weeks was given over to organising specialist courses for different crew members in subjects as varied as the innards of the watermaker to the electronics circuitry of the radar. Nearly all of this had to be done by each yacht on a self-help basis. The Challenge instruction was concerned more with the fundamentals of safety and life saving, such as advanced first-aid courses at the Royal Naval Hospital at Haslar.

None of the skippers had time for any life outside the Challenge and the crew. It was all consuming. Despite the moaning and groaning and the feeling that sometimes, through the summer, progress was illusory, learning was taking place and there was an indication of this even in the marina at Ocean Village. The ten Challenge yachts had been allocated possibly the smallest, tightest corner of the marina. Manoeuvring these 40 ton boats in and out was very difficult, yet by the end of the season based in Sou-thampton, as I confidently squeezed *Coopers & Lybrand* out between the other yachts and the veteran steamer *Shieldhall*, I wouldn't have recognised myself as the person who was hesitant at moving the boat 100 metres across the dock of Brixham marina.

Leg One:

September 1992 – November 1992

CHAPTER 4

First at the
Needles

During one of our routine training sessions I cockily told the crew that, for press coverage, there were only two important positions in this race: first out through the Solent past the Needles and first back into the Solent eight months later. Almost unbelievably we achieved the first of those ambitions. On 26 September we led the fleet out past those big white chalk cliffs and the feeling of achievement was just overwhelming. What a day!

The previous night had been the usual pre-race pandemonium – we were still trying to source spares and essential equipment for the boat late into the evening. Meanwhile, the crew and their families were milling around, heading off to hotels and restaurants saying their farewells. Many of the crew members, not just on our yacht, had families, parents or perhaps a girlfriend or boyfriend come down to wave them goodbye. At the same time the crew had important work to do on the boat and were torn between their true duties and loyalties. Skippers aren't immune to this problem either – Tony had come down to wish me well and to say a final farewell. He had become used to seeing me go off on yacht races and usually solved the problem by joining in the onboard work himself, but this time he had his parents with him. I was so busy with a thousand last minute details that they were kept waiting quite a while and there were the usual rows that couples on the eve of a farewell are often familiar with. By the end of the race I'd decided that Pete Goss had it about right with his decision never to have his wife and children at any of the starts.

On the following morning, the 14 crew of *Coopers & Lybrand* gathered on deck at 7.30 am. After all the goodbyes, packing, chatting and general organising, we were finally really off to do what we had been planning for nearly three years. It wasn't a day to lift anyone's spirits – a typical clammy, grey, autumn, English day. As we motored down Southampton water it even began to drizzle a little, hardly the kind of weather for the television and media spectacular that we had all half-anticipated. We knew from the level of press and television on the dockside that there was going to be an enormous amount of attention.

It was chaos in the starting area; hundreds and hundreds of boats almost as far as the eye could see. It was an amazing sight: line upon line of spectator craft, huge ferries, tall ships, the ten yachts themselves and sailors in their yachts, cabin cruisers, sports boats and inflatable dinghies. None of us on board could quite believe that we had generated this level of interest in the public.

I always get nervous in the 20 minutes before a start gun; if I tried to eat or drink anything I would probably physically throw up and this was the biggest race that I had ever seen or been involved in. If I was nervous, the crew were probably too absorbed and physically tired to be in the same condition. I decided that it would be a good idea to be well out of the mêlée an hour or two before the actual start, so we took the yacht eastwards up into the area of the forts to do some spinnaker practice.

After the chaos of departure from Ocean Village, the relief felt by all of us swept through the boat. At last we were free from the pressures of land life and we were about to start the adventure which we had all been preparing for during the last three years. We put the promotional spinnaker up first then practised a few gybes. Back at the starting area we practised a timed run to the start line. We'd all expected to see a lot of hullabaloo on the start line, but we were unprepared for the immense enthusiasm of the send-off.

It was apparent that the massive spring tide would have a great deal of influence at the start, pushing the yachts towards the line. My main concern was to make a good start without crossing the line too soon because that would incur a two hour time penalty.

Poised for the start, everyone had their positions and set jobs: on the foredeck were Matt, Neil and Maarten; John and Sam were at the mast; Richard manned the radio; primary winches were operated by David, Ann and Geraint; Robert was on the mainsheet; aft winches were operated by Brian and Murray; Titch was lookout and cockpit co-ordinator; finally, I was at the helm.

The pre-start manoeuvres had kept us all busy hoisting and

packing spinnakers; we had the lightweight race kite ready to go up. We delayed the hoist until we were sure that we would not arrive too early at the line. Once the gun had been fired by Princess Anne, it was 20 seconds before we crossed the line in fifth place. Three of the fleet had been caught out by the tide: *Commercial Union*, *Group 4* and *Heath Insured*. *Heath* also caught the start line buoy with her rudder.

To add to the drama of the first hour or two of the race, the Challenge had set up a contest whereby the first yacht to reach a gate a mile and a half from the start line won a £2000 cash prize with an identical prize for the first yacht to reach a second gate just off Cowes, slightly south and west of the starting area. The first leg was almost dead downwind in relatively light airs and with the volume of spectator boats criss-crossing the track in front of us, gybing three or four times in such a relatively short stretch of water was quite tricky. We reached the first gate in third position – just out of the money. After the turn we settled down on port gybe heading towards the second gate off Gurnard buoy. Ahead of us were *Pride of Teesside* and *Nuclear Electric*.

From Cowes onwards we crept down the island shore, the three yachts often within 50 yards of one another. The wind stayed light and we carried the spinnakers nearly to Hurst Narrows. This was where we made our break – and nearly struck disaster. *Pride of Teesside* opted for the north Channel route out of the Narrows and across to Christchurch. At that point there came a big wind shift; the previously fickle breeze went round to the south-west and was funnelled up the Needles Channel. We were the best prepared of the three yachts at this point – we had a genoa on deck ready to hoist – in contrast with *Nuclear Electric* and *Pride of Teesside*, neither of whom was quite as ready. But our forward planning nearly came to nothing. As we began to drop the spinnaker, a spectator boat, a small motor boat named *Puffin*, was coming towards us. We thought it would opt for the sensible course and pass up to windward of us, but at the very last moment, as we began to drop the spinnaker, he turned under our bow and down towards our lee side. I had to frantically luff up while the spinnaker halyard had already been released and the crew grappled with the spin-naker, bringing it in virtually over the stern. We missed the boat by about four feet, and probably a few of the passengers hadn't heard a woman using the kind of language I was directing towards them. The unkindest cut of all was a subsequent newspaper picture of the crew valiantly getting our spinnaker in, in difficult circumstances, but with a caption indicating that these rank amateurs barely knew what they were doing. But with no more than jangled nerves we settled down to find that we were the lead boat. First at the Needles, first out of the Solent – what a feeling!

Once the spectator fleet began to disperse and turn back eastwards towards the Solent there was a feeling of relaxation and relief aboard – the same atmosphere that you get on any racing yacht when the big drama of the start and the first hour or so is over. As we passed the Needles we felt as if we had already won the Challenge and the FA Cup rolled into one. If there had been the time we would have been hugging one another and jumping around on deck but there was too much to do. We had set our target of being first boat out through the Needles months ago and we'd done it! By next day, our first morning at sea together, it was back to reality. Perfection never lasts and we'd gone slightly off course during the night and been a bit slow with a couple of sail changes, so when dawn came we were lying fourth. We were heading for Ushant where we would turn south into the Bay of Biscay and ultimately the Atlantic. As we headed west, the breeze and the sea increased and by the time we reached Ushant both Brian and Robert were our first seasickness sufferers.

By Monday, our third day at sea, I think we were all beginning to feel a wave of mental and physical fatigue. It had been a gruelling week of preparation for the race, both emotionally and physically and now we had to get used to a watch system. We were out in the open ocean with steady winds of force 6 to 7 on the nose. This would be testing at the best of times so it was hardly surprising that we were tired, seasick and somewhat drained. Over the years, with other ocean races, I noticed that I often tended to develop a cold on the first day, perhaps the consequence of being overtired and vulnerable to infection. This race, the biggest of my life so far, was no exception.

One of the things I noticed very early on, was that as soon as I went on deck the behaviour changed. It was a rather 'teacher's here' mentality and I'm fairly sure it was the same on every boat. The crew were desperately anxious that everything should be 100 per cent right and equally sure that if it wasn't, 'Vivien would know it'.

We had begun a pattern of holding a crew meeting at 6.15 pm each evening just to update everyone on our position and navigation pattern. There was a continual desire from the crew to know what the overall plan was and it was often hard for me to keep explaining that the plan was to get to Rio in the quickest time, but that it might change almost hour by hour due to changing conditions. The crew, being inexperienced and lacking knowledge of navigation, often began to feel that I was holding something back and that there was some deeply strategic Master Plan that I was keeping secret from them. Sam, in particular, seemed to be unhappy that she didn't know exactly where we were or where we were heading. Although I found it an irritant to have to explain every nuance of the tactics and navigation, I could sense that this grumble was becoming a piece of grit in the communication between myself and the crew. I therefore made more effort to explain the weather and why we were going southwest at this particular time or perhaps turning slightly. The daily plots from all the other yachts were a help, especially as the most recent one showed that we were lying fifth – which was not too bad.

After four days at sea it was a pleasure to see the deck work getting quicker and better now everyone was settling down. I had a couple of days of suffering sore arms from doing too much steering across Biscay, but at this stage, in these heavier conditions few of the crew could steer for very long. It wasn't a lack of capability or willingness, but simply lack of stamina or the experience to helm for more than perhaps twenty minutes at a time. They were still tending to fight the boat rather than go with its motion. They all made mistakes, but few were as embarrassed as poor Geraint Lewis when he made an involuntary tack after forgetting he was holding a wheel and not a tiller.

Geraint had been crewing for me on the Sigma 33, and at his request had come out for a sail with us on *Coopers & Lybrand* on the last Sunday of Cowes week. He was clearly hooked on the idea of the Challenge and, as it was at exactly this time that Jill Ireland had decided to pull out, we were left with a space in the crew. Ann and Phil, the two regular crew on board that day, decided that Geraint was the boy for us – a suitable enough nutter to join *Coopers* – and worked quite hard to persuade him. By Tuesday of the following week he was phoning me from his job as a computer programmer and asking 'How do I get on the Challenge?' He had to pack into six weeks (in terms of fund raising and winding up the threads of his shore life), what the other crew members had done in three years. Small wonder that Geraint was sufficiently preoccupied in the early days of the race to put in the odd involuntary tack.

Our daily routine settled into a duty watch period of two hours sailing the boat, which involved helming, sail trim, writing the log and performing look-out duties. During the following two hours, this watch stood by to assist the duty watch with manoeuvres such as sail changes, tacks, gybes and reefs and making the drinks (hot chocolate was a persistently firm favourite, especially when we reached the Southern Ocean). Then came four hours off-watch – a time for eating, sleeping and generally relaxing. As skipper, I rarely had the chance to sit below doing nothing. I knew that on later legs we would be unable to sit around chatting; we would either be in the way or thrown around too violently. From Cape Horn to the Cape of Good Hope it would be a case of going off-watch and straight into your bunk.

After five days at sea, we were still finding out that we had forgotten things and left them ashore, or that the things we'd embarked were not quite what we wanted. Amongst the latter was some particularly dubious water embarked at Southampton. We began to use our yellow jerry cans for drinking water and then organised a rota of compulsory showers to use up the water in the two main tanks and refill it with clean water from our own watermaker. Meanwhile, we were still lying in fifth place and closing on the Spanish coast. We seemed to have been averaging a steady 160 miles a day, giving a boat speed of approximately 6.5 knots. We spotted another yacht for the first time since the evening of the start. Paranoia swept the boat as to whether it was another Challenge yacht and if it was, exactly *who* it was. Calm was restored when we realised it wasn't one of our rivals.

I was becoming aware that we needed to put more work and planning into our sail changes. Half the battle in any sail change is having the next correct sail ready on deck, ready to hoist. Some of my crew were taking the famous ten minute rule too literally. The rule dictates that when the weather alters enough to require a sail change, it is prudent to wait ten minutes before you actually make the change to see if the weather change is consistent. Unfortunately if you spend those ten minutes sitting and watching the sail, rather than getting the next sail up on deck, the ten minute rule becomes a twenty minute rule by the time you decide to change the sail.

Nearly a week at sea and we were still one of the most easterly positioned yachts. The weather had gone light and we had a frustrating time trying to squeeze the last bit of speed from the No. 1 yankee and full main. It was our first experience, since the Solent, of these light airs and as the day progressed it gave rise to frustration, a lack of concentration and also a lack of motivation. Our plan at this point was to stay fairly close to the Portuguese coast, although possibly not as close as *Interspray*, the most easterly yacht, which seemed to be heading for a barbecue on the beach. It had been a slow night for boat speed but a wonderful night for stories. Murray seemed to have led one of those lives full of incident and anecdote and, sitting on the leeward rail celebrating his 62nd birthday, he held the crew rapt for hours, even as the moisture dripped off the mainsail on to their heads, with his tales of life in Las Vegas.

It was a sign of the crew's increasing confidence that they began, fairly resolutely, to question my choice of sail selection. There is, however, no definitive right and wrong in these things – someone has to make the best choice they can and have the confidence to stick with that choice. You can't keep changing sails in light airs just because nothing seems to be working. The good side was that the crew *were* questioning – the down side was that inexperience made them frustrated as they were unable to accept that they weren't doing anything wrong. It was like coping with an occasional traffic jam on the way to work – sometimes you make things worse by ducking out of the traffic jam and taking a fifteen mile detour that takes longer than sitting there.

Not every decision of the skipper's is as weighty or debatable as sail changes. My word was also law when it came to loo paper. After just a week at sea we were already running low. Complex mathematics gave an outcome that we were going to be rationed to two sheets per visit, which met with hilarious and vociferous opposition from some aboard – three sheets were regarded as the minimum.

I think the reality began to dawn on some crew members that it was going to be a long time at sea. Still, there were simple pleasures such as the repeated delight in seeing dolphins. Even a change of diet cheered us – some vegetable burger mix with additional onions, corned beef and any other left over cooked meat was a great success; it was good to taste something fried – a day's break from 'the McDougalls breeze', as we had nicknamed the unfortunate side effect of our dried food diet.

The listing, purchasing and storage of food is one of the most difficult jobs on board any boat. As an example, allowing for three drinks per day for each crew member, we would need about 1500 tea bags for 5 weeks at sea. Sam and Robert worked very hard to organise effective sealed plastic packaging for most of the food. After sampling the dehydrated food during training, we decided to opt for it as our staple diet. It was relatively easy to store and very easy for everyone to prepare – just add water, heat and eat. We devised a 14 day menu which was repeated, mostly variations around pasta, rice and instant mashed potato. Mars bars provided treats and the cheesecake mix became a firm favourite.

We were now heading exactly south-west at 8.5 knots under spinnaker and were to stay under spinnaker for the next eight days. I decided that confidence, sail trim and motivation was so much easier to achieve with some wind. Also I still believe that the decision to stay east paid off in the long run and as the wind changed, as I predicted, I think my rating with the crew increased. At the daily inter-boat Chat Show we learned that *Interspray* had now got a decent lead on the whole fleet, but they were the most easterly boat and we were now in second place so our policy of staying inshore paid off.

After a week at sea the difference in competence and confidence in the crew was quite extraordinary. It was encouraging to see how capable they were becoming in all aspects of sail handling. For instance, we did a gybe peel from the three-quarter ounce kite (spinnaker) to the promo (promotional spinnaker) in 10 knots apparent (20 knots true breeze). We'd never done a peel, let alone a gybe peel on the yacht so it was quite a target to set ourselves. It took a while to set up; there was one crew briefing and a quick recap to show how everything worked, especially John Kirk's spinnaker net. The manoeuvre involved hoisting a second spinnaker inside the first, then releasing the old kite outside and recovering eighty feet of billowing sailcloth into the cockpit. If the peel was perfect, then it should also be dry. As well as keeping the sail dry, the aim is to keep maximum boat speed. Although we did get the sail a bit wet the first time, we had the added complication of gybing simultaneously. There were lots of rope and flailing arms and legs, but we managed it. This was certainly not a task we could have achieved just a week ago before the start, and that morning proved to be satisfying for everyone. The minus was that after a week of fresh air and hard work I still had a cold and retired to bed with Lemsip and snuffles.

It took us eight days to regain the lead we'd held at the Needles, but on the night of Sunday, 4 October we managed it. We'd been close to *Interspray* for some time; during the night we spotted her lights and then crossed a quarter of a mile ahead of her. I called skipper Paul Jeffes on the VHF and jokingly said it was time to hand over the yellow jersey (as in the Tour de France). The pressure was now back on us as we tried to maintain our lead. I also had a prearranged chat with Chay back at the base. They were obviously delighted with all the press and media coverage that the race was generating; the people following it must have been on tenterhooks as the lead had changed between five yachts in just the first week of racing. It was pretty exciting!

Downwind sailing gave the crew plenty of time for conversation. The game Pictionary was enthusiastically played, especially by Sam, John, Matt and Maarten. Maarten Malmberg was a 23 year old Dutch student who joined after sailing aboard *Coopers & Lybrand* on our promotional visit to Holland in June. His most frequent English words: 'very good, very good' delivered in an Arnold Schwarzenegger style of accent (hence the nickname 'Arnie'), had become almost the boat's catch phrase. After endless games of Pictionary I couldn't help wondering what his English would end up like.

When a day's run clocked up between 210 and 220 miles, morale was high, but complacency began to set in regarding the pace at which we were travelling and I needed to find ways of channelling the crew's high spirits. I had to convince them that it's easy being in the lead, but even easier to lose it. Personally, I reckon that it is the hardest position to be in in any race. I thought then that we had gone too far west and headed due south in an effort to compensate. To introduce a touch of competition, I posted up each day's run for every watch on the noticeboard. Immediately there were cries of unfair, and that adjustments should be made to allow for changed wind conditions for each watch and so on. But just how far can you take this kind of thing?

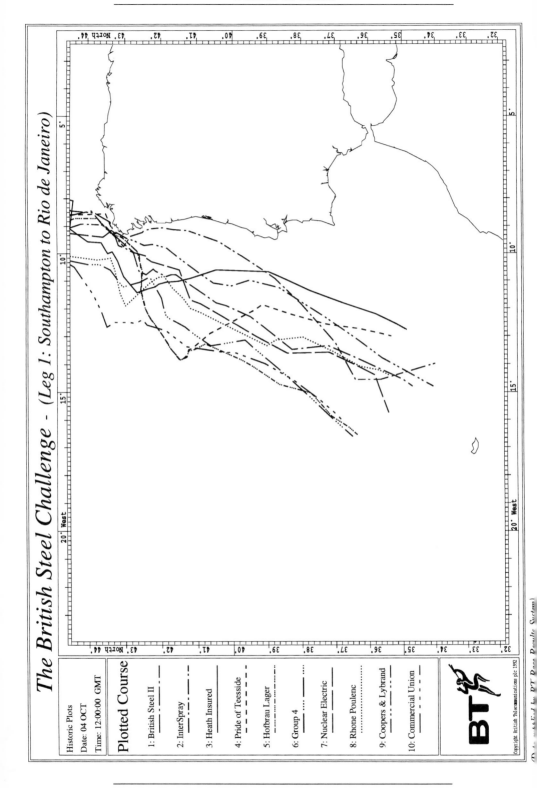

The British Steel Challenge - (Leg 1: Southampton to Rio de Janeiro)

Historic Plots
Date: 04 OCT
Time: 12:00:00 GMT

Plotted Course

1: British Steel II — · —
2: InterSpray — · · —
3: Heath Insured ——
4: Pride of Teesside — — —
5: Hofbrau Lager — · · · —
6: Group 4 · · · · · ·
7: Nuclear Electric ——
8: Rhone Poulenc · · · · · ·
9: Coopers & Lybrand — — —
10: Commercial Union — — —

BT

Copyright British Telecommunications plc 1992

Now that we were well away from UK weather forecasts we began to spend at least half our time chasing weather fax information. Norfolk, Virginia produced some good ones although it was a better signal at night. The art of tuning the weather fax signal from the SSB radio is to listen to the tone and tune it in until it's at its strongest.

We enjoyed the race reports that came up in the next few days – Chay loved headlines such as 'Only woman skipper in the lead'. What was normality eight days ago was never to be the same again; only the queue for the heads reminded me of life and people in general. We really were in the tropics now and even found a flying fish on our foredeck – our first of the trip. Brian cooked it and everyone had to have a taste. All we needed was the other 27 fish to make a full breakfast for the entire crew!

After four days in pole position we were just west of Tenerife when we realised that we had lost our lead to *Interspray*; we were disappointed, but not totally surprised. The most easterly yachts certainly had the edge, both in terms of wind and current.

It's still a surprise to me just how much time it took to coach each individual out of the 13 in the skills they needed to race the boat. We had now been at sea for nearly two weeks and I was pleased to be able to spend time with Murray to talk him through gybing the boat while driving. His comment was 'no-one ever explained to me how to do it before' as he referred to the method of balancing the yacht by driving it to keep the spinnaker full throughout the turn without letting the mainsail gybe back. It's always satisfying to help someone learn a new skill.

The next day saw us virtually drifting in the lightest of airs, but we had perfect conditions to deal with an unexpected man overboard drill. Geraint had been scrubbing the transom and had dropped the brush over the stern. We were doing probably less than a half knot and as the brush gently floated away he prepared to jump in and swim after it. I asked him to tie on the end of a lazy sheet as a safety line. Geraint obviously thought he could swim as quickly as a drifting scrubbing brush and jumped straight in. By the time he had reached the brush, grabbed it and turned around to look back at the yacht, we were already perhaps fifty yards away. He began to swim after us, but holding a scrubbing brush when swimming is not the easiest of tasks. When he stopped for a breather, the distance between us and Geraint was still increasing. There was no choice but to drop the spinnaker and bring the boat back on to the breeze in order to return upwind to collect a somewhat abashed and exhausted Geraint, plus scrubbing brush. As the light weather continued, tempers began to fray easily, but at least we had the distraction of amusing ourselves by making a lanyard for Geraint while he in turn made one for the deck brush.

CHAPTER 5

The Atlantic Wind Hole

As we sailed south-west, Robert and Richard in particular were putting more and more effort into making our weather fax system work. Because I had experienced some 'first-generation' weather fax machines some four years earlier, my own expectations of the system were not high. The crucial determinate of how useful the information is, is the clarity of the picture. We had a considerable left slip problem as the picture arrived on the screen. The operator was obliged to play the cursor, sometimes almost continuously, in order to keep the picture usable. Because we didn't know any better we thought it was always meant to be this hard and consequently didn't make any fuss about it or complain to Challenge headquarters. The first inkling we had that there was a general difficulty through the fleet was a questionnaire that came through from Challenge headquarters, asking us about our experience of using the weather fax machine and to comment on the clarity of the pictures received. On board *Coopers & Lybrand* we had no means of knowing that this was to prove to be a big controversy back in the UK – in fact we didn't find out until we arrived in Rio. Some of the sponsors were claiming that their yacht's equipment didn't work and other boats apparently had an unfair advantage in having gear that was providing clear information.

The newspapers, eager for any story about the Challenge, quickly seized on this first controversy of the race. Especially in Rio, this was the one topic that was creating some of the most heated and damaging discussions at the skippers' meetings. People would say 'It's all right for you, because your fax was working perfectly', which was the first I'd heard about it. Without seeing other data to compare the information we had against that of other boats, I would side-step the issue by saying 'Well it did us a lot of good. We finished ninth, so what's your problem?' With my technical background, I like to have data and facts to make comparisons. I was quite shocked that people could make this judgement without any factual back-up.

The discussion went on in Rio and the question arose as to whether we would carry weather faxes on the rest of the race. I still held the view that much of the problem stemmed from operator error. However, we felt we had fully learned the operation of our machine and there was still a flaw – but no one had come up with a plausible explanation as to what this fundamental flaw was. But that was all still in the future. At this point, what did concern me was whether to expect much reliable weather information for the two Southern Ocean legs where making the correct sailing decisions would heavily depend on having accurate weather information.

We had lost some distance on one or two other boats and were now no longer in the lead due to a compromise route through the Canary Islands which was chosen to cover both sides of the fleet. Four yachts went inside us to the east and another five were still to the west. One side would have given us more breeze, the other side should have provided a more favourable current. Our mistake was to plump for the middle and get nothing. This actually proved to be a bad tactical move as we went from first to last in about 26 hours. We sat in our own private 'hole', with no wind, remaining in that situation for the next four days. Everyone else was travelling faster than we were. With the frustration of virtually going backwards against the competition and rising temperature, tempers got very short. Add to that, 14 people living in close confinement in an oven-like steel hull, and the atmosphere became almost explosive. We resorted to a 'sense of humour failure' board. Only two failures were allowed per day – each was marked out of ten. David came top of the list when he was inadvertently awakened two hours early for his next watch; his shouts were so loud that they woke up everyone else! Fortunately after the inevitable comments and cartoon drawn on the board, David's sense of humour was restored.

We learned from the latest Chat Show that we were now nearly 200 miles behind the leaders, *British Steel II* and *Interspray*. The GPS gave our estimated time of arrival at Rio as 14 December, with

3346 miles still to go at our current speed. The most frustrating feeling was that we couldn't do anything about it (mind you, privately one tended to try to apportion blame). Part of the problem was that there was nothing or no one tangible to vent anger and frustration on – no wind, no speed, no other boats in sight – understandably the crew were very unhappy.

I decided to set them an achievable target: the boat speed must equal half the true wind speed. For example, we aimed for 3.5 knots in 7 knots of true breeze. It gave the crew something to aim for – if they could achieve that then they were not far off getting the best performance from the boat under those poor conditions. It proved to be a good system, but even though we tried our best we were still lying 262 miles behind the lead boats which were covering 100 miles in 12 hours compared to our distance of 45 miles.

There was gloom about the race but shouts of glee when we saw our first whale. It was a sperm whale, measuring about 35 feet long – half the size of the yacht – breaching about two thirds of its body out of the water. It appeared approximately 30 yards off the starboard side of the yacht. Everyone rushed to the rail to look, but by the time cameras were found all you could see was the disturbed water. As far as wildlife spotting went, we also saw turtles and a pair of sharks very close to the boat, and passed through a school of feeding dolphins, but not close enough to take photographs and identify the species. At the slow speed we were travelling at it was possible to fish, although fairly unsuccessfully. We had several bites but managed to lose half the line complete with lures and hooks.

As we headed towards the Equator, the weather stayed hot, clear and almost windless. As options were discussed as to how to cool off, I suggested diving from the spinnaker pole end with a sheet tied on at the waist and attached to the yacht for safety. Perhaps I should have kept quiet. Robert was the first to go for it – he climbed up the front of the mast and sat on top of the spinnaker pole, then edged his way to the outboard end before tying on. Neil and Geraint both tried it and then focused their attention on me, pointing out that it was my idea. I was not sure that I could manage the climb out on to the top of the pole by climbing up the downhaul, but I grimly realised that it had to be tried. I did make it but didn't feel too happy standing on the pole end which was very wobbly. It was probably the best photographed dive as everyone lined up to watch!

Day 16 and at last we had broken the 7 knot barrier for the first time in 4 days. Although we had a couple of spurts at 6 knots there was nothing lasting. We'd also put the promotional spinnaker up – another brilliant peel. Everyone on the boat became much happier now that we were moving at a steady speed, but we had a lot of catching up to do. There was a general perplexed feeling of it being unfair that the yachts to the west had moved faster when they were much closer to the centre of the high pressure system. Where were they getting that breeze from? Still, that's sailing; you either get too much or too little wind and it's always in the wrong direction. I felt that I should try to talk more with the rest of the crew about my plans, course, and what I required of them. I tried to follow the old presentation formula: overview; tell them what you are going to tell them; tell them; then tell them what you said; and then summarise. Perhaps I wasn't clear enough or maybe some of the crew practised selective listening.

We started closing the gap, gaining a few miles on those to the west and slowing up the gain from those ahead. Geraint, as the main man in charge of the engine, had been spending considerable time and effort trying to trace a mysterious oil leak into the bilge. Despite continually monitoring the level of oil in the engine and checking the seals and gaskets all around the engine block, there was no visible source of the leak. Eventually we tracked it down to a pin-hole in the five litre container of spare engine oil that was stowed in the bilge and was now empty. It was a waste of spare oil, but a huge relief that it was not a serious problem.

I'd began to plan a crossing of the Doldrums, which was to be our next hurdle. My planned entry point for the Inter Tropical Convergence Zone (ITCZ), as the Doldrums are technically known, was at 10°N, 25°W. From the weather information given out on the Inmarsat from the French station at Toulouse came the plot of the ITCZ. Whilst plotting this on the charts over a period of about five days it became apparent that this band moves as a wave formation and there are broader and narrower sections where one can cross the so-called Doldrums. By following this pattern carefully we were able to cross at one of the narrow stages.

We were then lying in seventh place. All the yachts to the west of us appeared to have started moving, although four of us were within 25 miles of each other on our 'distance to go' scale. I suspected that, by now, any advantage that the leading yachts had by being to the east had disappeared and we were fighting to hold our own. The heat was becoming uncomfortable; the humidity made sleeping nearly impossible. We managed to be well-rested, though, because the watch system allowed two hours sailing the boat, two hours on standby and then four hours off. However, we felt very hot and clammy all the time.

Our first indication of the Doldrums was a distant view of lightning. On the Chat Show the fleet were already beginning to refer to the Doldrums as a parking lot for 67 foot yachts. I had a dream vision of all the yachts floating out of the other side of Doldrums evenly positioned. However, the leading yachts were still well ahead.

During the early days whilst trying out various watch systems, we all agreed that some changes to the watch make up would help with passing knowledge around the boat. Half-way on this first leg we had been having an on-going discussion with regard to swopping people around in watches and some interesting views surfaced that I was previously unaware of. When I suggested that I was going to change the make-up of the watches everyone became very defensive. They thought they understood why I was doing it in general, but when it came down to specifics they became very uptight. I spoke to crew individually to see what their views were about the combinations and came up with, what was to me, a reasonable line up. However, when I started to implement it I realised that people can be very reluctant to accept change. At first they didn't want to know; they were very tense about it. But once we had carried out the change and it worked, they accepted it. One of the plans involved moving Brian, who was the third person on what we called the 'gooseberry watch'. It acquired its name because Neil and Ann were getting very close and spending a lot of time with each other, to such an extent that they became far less involved with other crew members – a situation which threatened the team element. When the change took place I think the crew were surprised that it didn't divide the clique pairings as much as they had thought it would. After the reorganisation, the watches were as follows: Neil, Ann and Richard; Matt, David and Maarten; Rob with Murray and Brian and John with Sam and Geraint. When the final change was announced, John made everyone laugh by announcing 'That's great, we've got big mouth, big nose and big tits all on the same watch'!

As a further romantic connection, Titch the mate, had his girlfriend Sue on board *Commercial Union*; they had chosen to be on separate boats. Although they obviously spoke to one another about what was going on aboard the other's boat, they seemed to be very discreet so we never had any fears that our tactical secrets were going to *CU*. Nevertheless, it created a situation where you felt you never really knew where you were. Alongside in Rio, for example, our maintenance programme had to be turned on its head to accommodate *CU*'s arrival. In the battle for loyalties I felt that the boat lost. Hindsight, always infallible, makes me think that perhaps they would have been better off on the same boat.

By now, inevitably, nicknames had started to emerge. Richard became universally known as 'Bertie' from a reference to Jeeves and Bertie Wooster. Another parody which was followed enthusiastically was likening crew to characters from 'Dad's Army'. John, after excitedly shouting 'Don't panic, don't panic', became known as 'Jonesy'. Matt, with his background in the Territorial Army, was quickly dubbed 'Pike', while the dour Scot Robert became, of course, 'Fraser'. At one point, Geraint became known as 'Martini' because Brian, on trying to wake him, then informed the watch at changeover that Geraint had been 'shaken but not stirred'.

We'd chosen a southerly course but the wind was forcing us to make more westing than we really wanted to. The crew were still obsessed with following a compass course rather than aiming for the best speed and direction they could manage. I felt sure that this would improve during the following months, but it was very difficult to keep boredom at bay. I still had the idea that the overall group feeling was that they were there for a 'sail-around-the-world.' The race side interested them and they certainly wouldn't want to finish last, but the competitive element with consequent dedication to continual sail trim (what I always referred to as the 'trim loop') was still largely absent. Maybe it was my fault for not keeping them 'geed up' at all times.

The trim loop comes from a North Sails handbook and runs as follows:

> *Mainsail* 1) Set twist with mainsheet tension.
> 2) Set depth with mast bend/outhaul/flattener.

3)   Set draft position with Cunningham.

4)   Set helm balance with traveller position.

5)   Finally go back and fine tune the total power of the main with above controls, or reduce power by reefing.

Genoa 1)   Determine overall power by selecting correct genoa.

2)   Determine efficiency of genoa with lead angle (car position).

3)   Set depth twist with sheet tension.

4)   Set depth and twist with fore-and-aft lead position.

5)   Set draft position with halyard tension.

All the westerly yachts had now caught up with us except *Commercial Union*, and the leading three yachts were well ahead. The crew actually caught their first fish – Bertie and Robert landed a six pound barracuda which, after very little discussion, was filleted and baked. It was afterwards that the rumour began; someone had read about a special type of barracuda that is toxic and not good for eating. However, it appeared that they had landed the edible sort – just a bit chewy.

On 19 October, preparations were under way for crossing the Equator on the following day. Unfortunately my knee caught a bad twist that morning so I put a brace back on it. It was the second time I had suffered with it during this leg and it was causing me real concern – and pain. Cartilage damage had been diagnosed about a week before the start; I believe I had injured it originally whilst dinghy sailing in Toppers out of Brixham in April. However, it didn't really manifest itself until the stress of continual sailing started causing problems. On this occasion I was in the galley balancing gently when the knee twisted – you don't have to be on deck to have this difficulty. It began to be a real problem and this was just the gentle stage of the race. The knee-brace became an object of hate and torture, especially in the heat. It also tended to cause the ankle and foot to swell up very badly. Living with the pain and discomfort made me less communicative and I was, on occasion, very short with one or two of the crew. Even skippers have off-days, although I'm not sure if that's allowed.

We knew 20 October was going to be a big day for us. Earlier

I had begun to head the boat towards the east in the hope of picking up the south-east trade winds. That had worked in as much as we had moved up from our ninth position and expected to be the fifth boat to cross the Equator and enter the Southern Hemisphere. Aboard *Coopers & Lybrand* we began preparations for the crossing-of-the-line ceremony. John Kirk was cast as 'Father Neptune' with Robert as his assistant (both appropriately costumed). Their traditional duty is to cleanse the initiates inside and out – some goo had to be eaten on a biscuit, followed by a dousing with a particularly vile brew of cold curry over everything. Afterwards, the boat was caked and then well and truly baked with this mess. We hove-to so that we could go for a swim off the stern to clean bodies and hair and sluice a lot of water over the deck to clean it. It became apparent that debris from this mess was going to be reappearing all over the place for the next week. As the yacht was still drifting at 3 knots, we had a lot of lines over the stern and getting back on board was really quite difficult. After the messy bit we properly celebrated with champagne and Sam's mum's Christmas cake. It was eaten with relish and promptly re-named 'Equator cake'.

Lying in my bunk later in the day, I was furious to hear a conversation from the cockpit between the crew on watch to the effect that sail trim did not seem to make any difference to this boat. They could appreciate that this amount of sail trim on a half-tonner round the Solent obviously worked because of the closeness of the racing but they felt that out here in the middle of the ocean, sail trim wasn't really important. I couldn't let this pass. I went straight up on deck to explain to the crew that although a big and heavy boat like this wouldn't respond right in front of their eyes to sail trim, it was extremely important to maximise the boat speed. Speed could be lost very quickly and, with a boat of this size and displacement, it could take five or ten minutes for it to get back up to full speed.

I couldn't help thinking, 'If that's their attitude, no wonder we're ninth'! The feeling re-emerged that I had a crew that were just happy to 'sail round-the-world'. Racing was all very well but the dedication and concentration required to maximise boat speed was a complete anathema to them. Later in the day I had a session with the watch leaders to try to imprint on their brains what I felt was the importance of sail trim.

The next day was terrific sailing weather with 18 to 20 knots of breeze enabling us to close reach. Looking at the crew made me realise that, despite yesterday's small confrontation, the situation was still improving by leaps and bounds only three weeks after our departure from Southampton. Taking just the incident on the previous day where the crew had to haul themselves out of the water after the 'Father Neptune' swimming session; earlier in the race two or three of them would not have had the strength to do it.

We then had 1590 miles to go – at the current rate of progress, I estimated that it should take us about seven to eight days. I instinctively wanted to start driving the boat harder, but it always ended up being a compromise. I couldn't do every bit of trim myself and the crew had never operated at that level of intensity before. I still had very little feedback from the crew and I wondered whether I had really made myself that unapproachable or were people still worried that they were doing something wrong? Their defence mechanism was still very strong. I hoped that they would begin to open up, which would predispose them to learn quickly. Robert, Brian and Matt were all looking carefully at things and trying new methods which was a good sign. At times I found Ann hard to understand. She adopted a very aggressive front some-times – maybe connected with being dubbed 'the watchleader's girlfriend'. There were also comments from other crew members that she had become a little bossy, but without the backup of knowledge, mainly assuming that her ideas or perhaps what she has been told by Neil was correct. It was a tricky situation. I could do little about it except perhaps let the rest of the crew sort her out. As a crew member, Ann worked hard at everything and had learnt a lot from scratch but she now seemed to have hit a plateau in the learning curve.

It is always important, on long passages, that tensions between the crew find a release through humour rather than anger. We already had a sense of humour failure board, Pictionary, a Mars bar eating competition and now we instituted a 'limerick com-petition day'. The limerick was to be about the next person to you in height – for instance I had to do Ann; Ann did Paul and so on through the heights. I had half expected that a good deal of the fun would come from trying to guess the heights of everyone, but Geraint compiled a list with great precision.

Ode to Arnie written by Matt
Each day in the galleys he stood
After seconds of dinner and pudd
The bowl is too small, almost nothing at all
But the cheesecake I think very good.

Limerick by Ann to Brian
There was a butcher called Bird
Who became the boat's medic we heard
He's sharp with his knife
So watch out for your life
The best cure is never to get hurt.

Limerick about Murray written by David
There once was a sailor from Nevada
Who joined Chay Blyth's armada
From Southampton to Rio with Elan and Brio
Such a shame he's going no farther
(Murray was just doing the first leg).

Limerick to Matt from Geraint
There was a young sailor called Matt
Who climbed masts like a turbo-charged cat
He could whizz to the hounds
And absail back down
While the boat was still going full chat.

Limerick about Titch by Geraint
A mariner whose name was Paul
Was always on watch or on call
But apart from to nag or to smoke a quick fag
He was seldom on deck, if at all.

CHAPTER 6

Rio in Sight

Spirits were fairly high after the limerick competition and we began to seriously prepare for our arrival in Rio. The crew started taking malaria tablets and an 'alongside' job list started to grow. As early as a week away, paperwork began to appear – there were damage reports for Challenge headquarters, and inventory lists to complete. Titch and Brian filled out a spreadsheet; they made a distinction between all the items we had in the store and those that we should have had, but hadn't – plus what we'd used or had broken. After the chaos of the start we had left without items such as storm boards and spare battens which we really did need aboard.

For the previous couple of weeks Sam had been complaining of 'nappy rash', an affliction which tends to bother all sailors sitting around in damp, salty clothing for long periods of time. Even I was beginning to suffer from the same syndrome. However, a Thousand-Miles-To-Go party complete with a bottle of scotch was enough to take my mind off my backside. Everyone was really happy and bright or were they just drunk? The spinnaker take-down went well. It was now so hot that it was virtually impossible to sleep off watch so the boat was full of very tired people.

My crew were still too fixed on sailing a compass course. When the helm was handed over, subsidiary instructions such as course boundaries and the need to steer the boat fast, rather than sticking to a fixed three digit number seemed to get lost in the hand over. I tried to impress on them the importance of way-point closing velocity (WCV) as well as simple speed through the water. The display for the WCV was below at the GPS station on *Coopers* and the helmsman couldn't actually see it; two other yachts had fixed repeaters for this data mounted on deck visible to the helmsman.

This breach of the spirit of the rules was to become a contentious issue in Rio.

Up to this point there had been no major personality clashes amongst the crew. One thing that emerged was that they all wanted to do a bit of everything, rather than concentrate on learning one particular task well. Although we had allocated specialist duties to each person there wasn't an overwhelming willingness to learn and become expert at that particular skill.

Communications between myself and the mate Titch were not perfect. It culminated in a 1 am discussion on safety aboard the boat. Admittedly, it wasn't a perfect time to be holding such a conversation and if we had been communicating better we probably would not have had such a talk at this time. Titch seemed to feel quite strongly about a couple of safety issues, one of which was the carrying of personal emergency beacons at all times. This was a good idea, but to set new boat policy at 1 o'clock in the morning with one or two watches without advising the skipper is not really the best way of implementing it. I think Titch was feeling the strain of being mate rather than 'one of the boys' and was beginning to get a bit worried about the organisation of all the stores and getting ready for Rio. It is my nature to pull a problem back inwards and solve it myself, which made it difficult for me to successfully resolve situations involving other people such as my working relationship with Titch. Ideally I prefer to be more pro-active than re-active, so I wondered why, at that moment, I was not.

The list of jobs and inventory items that we'd prepared in advance for arrival in Rio eventually ran to some 4 pages of my A4 daybook and numbered 60 items. The list was incredibly diverse, ranging from a new dustpan and brush to calibration of the barometer. We had always expected the first leg to be relatively straightforward – it was to be the longest period at sea for most of the crew and, in many respects, it was regarded as a training leg for what was to come. After around 30 days at sea we had, generally speaking, a pretty happy crew, but there was an undercurrent beginning to develop of thinking that it was easy. The group really had no idea of the bad weather to come. Perhaps due to the lack of extreme physical challenge on the first leg, many of the crew still harboured the old doubts about how they would handle what was to come – especially when we looked at the weather charts with lots of very tight isobars which meant a lot of breeze. Some of the weather charts we received covered a relatively large area – from our position slightly south of the Equator down to the deep south Atlantic – and we could see the weather systems down there that we would encounter on the next leg and beyond. With less than 24 hours to go to Rio, the crew were naturally beginning to think of shore-side activities. John Kirk was already dreaming of windsurfing.

At this stage we were still lying ninth, approximately 60 miles behind *Nuclear Electric* and approximately 25 miles behind *Rhone-Poulenc*. I knew from the experience of the yachts that had already finished that there was a substantial calm patch in the bay off Rio harbour and also along the coastal section preceding Rio itself. We had been plotting the two boats immediately ahead of us and it was obvious that they were going slowly, so we decided to stay between five and ten miles farther off shore and go a little south as we came towards Rio. We made our approach through the early hours of the morning, fine reaching under a lightweight spinnaker. Our first glimpse of the city was the lights of Corcavado – the statue of Christ on the mountain top above the city and then the lights of Copacabana beach came into view.

As dawn came we saw *Rhone-Poulenc* inshore of us and not moving, which must have been a worry to them as they looked back and saw us under spinnaker. Further on we saw *Nuclear Electric* so close inshore that they were practically on the beach; we could see them against the buildings. It later emerged that skipper John Chittenden had spent most of the night anchored in a totally becalmed sea. We carried the breeze into the finish line, but both the rival yachts ahead of us were able to pick up their share of it, *Nuclear Electric* finished in seventh place, 22 minutes ahead of us, and *Rhone-Poulenc* was eighth, just 7 minutes ahead of us. After 5300 miles of racing from Southampton, the fact that three boats finished within half an hour of one another made exciting racing. Even more incredible was that the three boats that had come in fourth, fifth and sixth the previous afternoon off Copacabana Beach had finished within 90 seconds of one another!

As soon as we had crossed the finish line the sails were lowered and we hurried to clear the decks for the welcoming party. Several of us then disappeared to change into our crew uniforms, previously forgotten in the tense, close finish.

We found a suitable anchorage in the bay adjacent to the yacht club. Guests then arrived; Chay, armed with a bottle, was one of the first to congratulate us; this set a pattern for the end of all the legs.

There was insufficient depth of water for the Challenge yachts to lie alongside the Rio Yacht Club so we were anchored off about 300 metres from the quay. It was the first time the mainsail had been down for 31 days. All on board *Coopers & Lybrand* were delighted to be there, if a little apprehensive at the prospect of going into a 'strange' environment. We celebrated with champagne at 8 am (and chocolate milk for Robert who's teetotal). Sugar Loaf mountain in real life is still as impressive as it is in pictures.

My first task was to get ashore, see to the administration and visit the Challenge office. As the yacht's container had not arrived, I went off to the hotel with Greg Bertram, Challenge MD and retired to the bar. I was very impressed by the Yacht Club of Rio; it stretches for nearly a mile along the waterfront. Apparently 20 per cent of the large membership are interested in sailing, the rest are social members. The long, low terraced bar and restaurant on the verandah became a natural focal point for the thirsty crews and skippers.

My other urgent appointment was with some knee specialists. After two and a half hours, the doctors' verdict was cartilage damage but there wasn't enough time to do anything about it in Rio. They gave me a regime of exercises to keep muscle tone and I was told to keep wearing the brace. The Challenge were very helpful in organising the medical attention; they promised to contact UK doctors to see what the necessary surgery involved and to see if it could be arranged for Hobart when we arrived there. Chay was slightly worried that it might actually put me out of the race – *but not a hope*!

Six and a half days after we reached Rio, *Commercial Union* finally arrived in tenth place and completed the Challenge fleet. I'd known, during the previous summer, that skipper Will Sutherland had been under the same sort of scrutiny that I had gone through. Coming in so far adrift of the fleet there were bound to be problems on board. The crew were angry and unhappy. That was shown graphically by some little cameo acts at the drinks party after they'd finished. A crew member with a white stick and the sign 'Navigator' around his neck, blundered around the party area tripping over boxes and crates. It was cruel but it relieved the understandable feelings of the crew of *Commercial Union*. Chay Blyth acted quickly and Will Sutherland was sacked and gone from Rio within two days of *Commercial Union's* arrival – a new skipper, Richard Merriweather was appointed.

Rumours were circulating around the Yacht Club waterfront that another skipper might go. I questioned Chay to try to get a bit more information in a joking fashion and said I'd heard a rumour that someone's seen Clare Frances walking around and did he have something to give me? Like my airline ticket home? He seemed to find this very amusing especially when I followed it with 'Well it looks like the tenth skipper has gone and I'm ninth so who's next?' John O'Driscoll who had finished eighth on *Rhone-Poulenc* was, in fact, then replaced by Peter Phillips, further endorsing my concern about being placed ninth. The rumour mill at the Yacht Club in Rio de Janeiro was so intense that every hour one of my crew would come up with yet another story. I told them that as far as I knew I wasn't going to be replaced as skipper and it wasn't our problem and we should do our very best not to get drawn into it.

The importance of the race almost took the Challenge itself unawares. It was initially a challenge to sail round the world, but became a fully serious race from the sponsors' point of view. The media attention partly created this atmosphere. The Challenge was very happy to receive any kind of publicity, whether it was generated by sponsors, crew volunteers or anyone else.

Lack of information and equipment underlined the difficulty that the Challenge office was having in this foreign port. Coopers and Lybrand, Brazil, helped us as much as they could with supplies and equipment. The day before the race restarted, Brian and William Ballantyne, Coopers' senior partners from the Rio office, went shopping for tools, pliers, small drill bits and files. Domingos Faria, president of Coopers, Brazil was a wonderful host; a keen yachtsman himself, Domingos became an enthusiastic Challenge race supporter. At the last minute he gave us the socket set from his own yacht as, whilst changing a damaged stanchion, we discovered that part of ours didn't float!

The saga of the weather faxes continued and began to hot up. Some sponsors were really upset by the notion that their boats had been disadvantaged by non-working equipment which, they believed, had functioned properly on other boats. Bob Fisher, a well known yachting journalist had been particularly dogged in pursuing this issue on the pages of the *The Guardian. Coopers & Lybrand* became a central part of the whole controversy because after we arrived in Rio, the consensus belief ashore was that our weather fax had worked – and indeed was the only one that had worked during the first leg. We were able to tell them that, in fact, ours had the same problem as all the other machines, but that three or four of our crew had become exceptionally good at operating it in such a way that enabled them to receive data. Thus we became the acknowledged 'experts' on the actual operation of the weather fax machines and as the controversy rumbled on we became a sort of bench mark for the whole question.

Andrew Roberts at the Challenge base did realise early in the race that there was a technical fault in the machines themselves and had ordered replacements. As race organiser, Chay was

OPPOSITE: ABOVE Father Neptune, alias John Kirk, and assistant Robert Faulds feeding the vile, gooey 'Equator cake' to Titch for 'internal cleansing'. David, having already been initiated, is filming.

BELOW Bertie and his barracuda – the first fish caught on the voyage. Brian is helming while Murray (left), Robert and Sam look on.

Page 70

ABOVE LEFT Almost seasonal, even though there were no fairy lights.

ABOVE RIGHT The hat party just prior to Cape Horn.

BELOW Ann taking the plunge from the spinnaker pole end. We were always seeking novel ways to take a swim.

Page 71

ABOVE Me helming on the emergency tiller. Never buy a 67 foot yacht without a wheel!

BELOW Brian is at the helm as we pass an iceberg off the Argentine coast; a wondrous sight, although feelings change when it's foggy and blowing a gale.

Page 72

ABOVE The party starts here as we dock in Cape Town.

BELOW LEFT The true extent of the damage to Coopers & Lybrand's *mast was fully revealed alongside the quay in Hobart. The graffiti was just some fun as we crossed the finish line.*

BELOW RIGHT The morning after the night before when we arrived in Cape Town; this ocean racing is so tough!

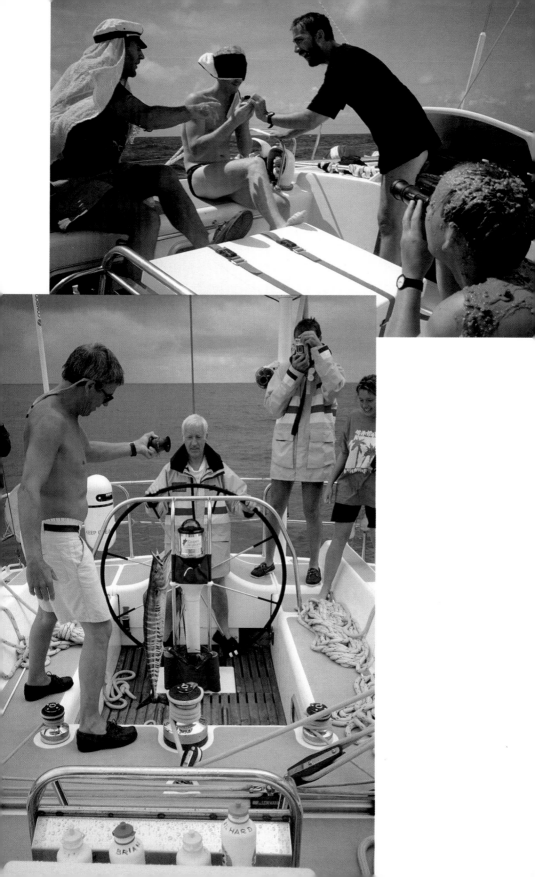

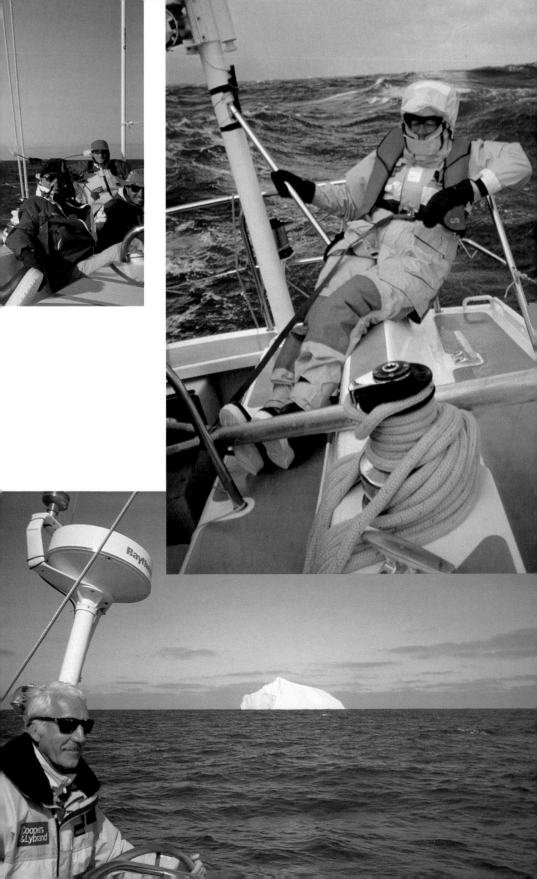

anxious to avoid internal warfare between angry main boat sponsors who had the impression that their yacht was being disadvantaged. To that end he asked that all skippers would accept new weather faxes and sign a declaration, before the start of the next leg, to the effect that they agreed to take them and accepted that they were working to an acceptable standard. Effectively, it gave any individual skipper, who was unhappy with the equipment he had been issued with, veto power over the issue of weather faxes. It was fundamental to the very concept of the One Design race that all the equipment had to be equal.

This became a very emotional issue as the weeks in Rio rolled by. In fact, on the morning of the start of the next leg, a skippers' meeting was convened at 9 am to secure agreement on the weather fax issue from the skippers. However, Mike Golding of *Group 4* had still not received a satisfactory picture on the weather fax aboard his yacht and was in communication with his crew via a hand-held VHF radio as the meeting progressed. On a slightly different tack, Richard Merriweather, the new skipper of *Commercial Union* was having SSB reception problems and was asking for special dispensation to receive direct weather information to his yacht from the Bracknell Met Centre via Inmarsat. Still faced with a lack of consensus amongst the skippers, Chay adjourned the meeting. As Chairman of the meeting, Chay was in typically bullish mood and told us in no uncertain terms that there was going to be a decision by 10.30 am, come what may. With two skippers still withholding their consent he decided that the new weather faxes would be taken from all the yachts, the start would be delayed and we would sail without the equipment. As we left the meeting room, Mike Golding's VHF crackled into life and he heard news from his crew that they had received an acceptable weather fax picture on their equipment. He then agreed to take it. It was a very difficult situation but once nine skippers agreed, it did not take long for us also to reach a consensus that, under strictly controlled conditions and via the Challenge, Richard Merriweather could receive the information from Bracknell.

On the organisational front, it was a major pain to have the yachts anchored off the Yacht Club rather than alongside a pontoon or jetty. As we didn't have our own dinghy, we had to rely on a water taxi service to take us to and from the boat. With over 100 crew trying to get backwards and forwards to the Yacht Club there was certainly peak period congestion. The boat taxi drivers became laden with beer, T shirts, hats; any bribe that might buy preferential treatment to avoid a long wait.

Although we were now in port, sail changes were still part of our life. The Challenge decided to take away our promotional spinnakers and replace them with asymmetric kites. During the summer of training before the race started, six kites had been damaged in the Fastnet race alone. Chay obviously became worried about spinnaker damage and felt that a heavier weight of sail would be appropriate for the middle two legs of the race. Chay was clearly also anxious that on the final leg of the race especially on the run up the Solent to the finish – with the eyes of the world on the Challenge fleet – the sponsors' spinnakers should be in one piece and clearly visible.

Social life ashore was absolutely unrelenting. Rio has its own time clock – one where eating, drinking and partying take place all night and the morning does not exist. Unfortunately, there were days when the mornings very much did exist, when we were scheduled either for corporate sailing days or I was committed to a skippers' meeting. The sailing was fine indeed. Amidst chaos and very difficult shoreside conditions it was a very pleasant feeling to get back to sea again, even though it was just for one day's corporate sailing. I really missed sailing and longed to get back into the routine.

During the Rio stopover we were looked after very well by both our sponsors with meals, trips out and assistance from the office. Richard Tudor of *British Steel II* and myself were invited to visit a mine by one of our sub-sponsors, Campanhia Vale de Rio Doce (CVRD), who supply British Steel with iron ore. The mine was in the heart of the Amazon forest and we were stunned by the beauty of the landscape, such a contrast to the ocean scenery that we had experienced. The visit to the Carajas mine, one of the largest open cast operations in the world, was fascinating and Penhair Carlotti, CVRD's representative, treated us as VIPs, providing superb hospitality. I found it strange to think that we had sailed about 5500 miles in 5 weeks to get to Rio and yet one could still travel for 2000 miles (by air) to reach the centre of Brazil – this was indeed a *very* vast country.

At the Challenge prize-giving party held at the Yacht Club around the swimming pool there was an amazing spread, with a full sit-down buffet complete with band and Samba dancing girls. After the girls' first dance, Brian and Richard went and borrowed two head-dresses and came out bare chested copying the Samba. It was immensely funny and none of the other crews' antics managed to cap it. We certainly partied hard but there was still a lot of work to be done, especially the provisioning of the yacht for the longest leg between Rio and Hobart.

Shopping for the boat's provisions caused endless amusement although very time consuming for Robert and Sam. The first test, travelling around in a taxi, was to find a large supermarket. The translation of labels on tins and packets was greatly helped by some of the local girls from the office of Coopers & Lybrand. The assistance we had in interpretation probably solved a number of potential problems. On one of the other yachts, *Interspray*, Ali Smith thought she'd bought tinned butter, but during the second leg it turned out to be very sweet tinned butterscotch! Sam was in charge of stores and felt very fed up because little help was forthcoming. We managed to get most of the food stowed away after throwing it from the dock on to the yacht – stowed maybe not to Sammy's plan, but at least keyed so she knew where to find it. My impression of her during this stopover was that she was searching for a confidante, a special close friend; this had first struck me months before, at the team-building weekend. When people were asked what they were looking for, words came up like 'loyalty' and 'confidence' – but Sam was looking for someone close. I didn't think she'd necessarily find what she was looking for either in Rio or on the Challenge – that's the type of friendship that either grows or just happens.

Leg Two:
December 1992–
January 1993

CHAPTER 7

The Iceberg Watch

On the morning of the start from Rio everybody was up very early. We organised groups to clean the bottom of the hull as far as they could reach. Jock Wishart who had flown out to Rio to give me physical and moral help, carried out the role of major diver, going down and cleaning the bits next to the rudder and the skeg as he wouldn't let anyone else go into the foul water. We also stuck six-inch strips of Dacron along all the seams on the mainsail. This was to give added strength to the single set of sails allowed by the Challenge for the whole race around the world. We needed to preserve our sails as carefully as possible. The aim was to tape up both sides of the seams, but we ran out of time and Dacron tape and only managed to get one side completed. We hoped that this would give us an advantage in boat speed in the final leg when possibly everybody else's mainsails were more tired and stretched than ours.

After a two and a half week balmy stopover in Rio, we wouldn't have been surprised if the start had been in very light air, but on the day there was a reasonable sailing breeze and the start itself was set as a reach. The first mile and a half to the fairway buoy was just off the breeze, not quite a beat. There was a certain amount of confusion in the hour before the start as we tried to locate the right VHF channel that everyone could communicate on. Once that was solved, with about 15 minutes to go, we had a closer look at the line. The pin end was always going to be busy and it looked as if it might be quite dangerous to be there with boats coming in fast and trying to harden up at the last minute. There is always a risk that you will get pushed out at the buoy. The other end of the line was towards land with little breeze, so we planned to be about four boat lengths from the pin end, coming in already trimmed for the first leg course and, hopefully, going at full speed at the right time. It worked reasonably well but we did get shadowed by *Hofbrau Lager* who then took our breeze and slowed us down a bit. We managed fourth round the windward mark.

The start was very tight, although I tried to convince myself beforehand that in a 9000 mile sailing leg, two or three seconds at the start isn't going to make any difference. The contest was such that *Interspray* was actually half a second over the line at the gun and there was a pin end collision where *Nuclear Electric* was coming in on course for the first mark and *Heath* and *Group 4* were trying to squeeze in the gap between *Nuclear* and the buoy. At the last minute *Heath* had to avoid the buoy and unfortunately his stern hit *Nuclear Electric*. Once round the mark, three or four boats quickly put up their new asymmetric spinnakers and went further off to the southwest, whilst a group of six of us stayed more directly south.

The crew were generally quite happy to be back at sea. This was, after all, what they had paid their £15,000 for. There was also a slight mood of trepidation – Cape Horn and the Southern Ocean lay ahead. It was understandable to be nervous and a little frightened. The duration of the leg was also a worry to some – our planning was for a leg of 60 days, which is a long time at sea.

After a few weeks ashore it was bound to take a while for the sea legs to re-establish themselves. The wind had freshened up and kicked up a reasonably big swell. It seemed like great sailing weather to me after Rio, but one or two crew members were finding it tricky. Sam, Brian and Phil were our sickies and even John was having difficulty in cooking and staying down below. I really hoped that this *mal de mer* was not recurring and that once the real gales and discomfort came in two or three weeks none of us would be afflicted by seasickness. I knew it was a worry to Sam and Brian particularly, although neither of them were as sick as they used to be.

Phil Jones was our single legger from Rio to Hobart. He was a steel worker from Port Talbot in South Wales and an experienced dinghy and J24 sailor. Phil was six feet four inches tall, very fit and had done quite a bit of sailing. He was to be one of our strongest men, certainly forward of the mast, and had knowledge of sail trim and the competitive drive to want to do well.

Neil had injured his hand during the last few days in Rio. We were moving the boat and decided to leave the anchor and chain buoyed with a fender for later retrieval. At the crucial moment of dropping the chain over the bow, the chain caught on the bow roller pin and trapped Neil's hand. It was a shame that the pin was on the wrong side relative to the forestay. If the angled part had been to starboard then the chain wouldn't have got caught – it was unfortunate, also, that Neil happened to be left-handed. He became a very solid watch leader – he had his own way of doing things and some of the crew found his set ways a bit inflexible, but understandable. He went through an unfriendly phase towards the rest of the crew when the relationship with Ann was first developing, probably being slightly defensive as everyone was. Neil was one who originally didn't want to sail with me and, even after the Fastnet practice race, would have taken a risk with a reserve skipper – although he did say to Chay that if I stayed he'd back me. He'd certainly done that and I think he grew to respect and possibly even to like me. Neil was very determined to do well and to do things properly and safely. He would always finish a job once he had started. His nickname aboard was 'spindly trucker' – his CV gave his profession as HGV driver.

One aspect of the Challenge that I felt strongly about was crew motivation and attitude. Because someone was paying for the opportunity to take part in the Challenge, was their attitude bound to be different from a sailor who does it for love *or* money? Some of the crews believed they were special and that the whole race was a bit of a breeze, because if things got difficult they could go 'sick' and the skipper would be there to sort it out. I think it would have been an improvement if, during the two years of training, the crew volunteers had been set specific goals to achieve in terms of both sailing ability and the whole ethos of running a yacht. A 'Beast' had been created by giving this opportunity of a lifetime to ordinary people. Not many of them were self-motivated enough to have completed a challenge like this on their own. There would probably always be this difference of attitude and perception between the skippers, who were self-motivated and who had always gone for challenges or races and the crew volunteers, who were all workers and high achievers but who needed a vehicle to achieve something like this. Then the 'Beast' changed; it became a race, requiring a completely different, competitive attitude, and one that very few of the crews would understand until the finish.

We were five days into the leg before I managed to get all the crew together at the same time. I wanted to have a discussion about timing of watches and also raise points such as general procedures concerning deck work, sail handling and sail changes. The crew were now doing the right things, but sometimes in the wrong order, which can make the job more difficult. They had the basics; it was just a question of tightening up skills to perform them quicker and better. It had to become habit, because in the conditions we were going into you had to be able to follow those procedures when cold, tired and wet. We also had to adjust the lifejackets; they were inflating when a wearer on the foredeck was struck by a wave. It was becoming a nuisance and we didn't have enough spare inflation cylinders to let this carry on. We took the automatic inflation off the lifejackets, leaving them with a tag you could pull to inflate or blow up by mouth in the traditional way.

Six days into the leg and we were in fifth position. Bracknell was providing a five day forecast which was passed to the race HQ and then relayed to us via Inmarsat but it was proving difficult to work out what was happening from these forecasts. I'd worked out a tactical plan for the next three days based on forecasts from Bracknell. At that time we received a very clear weather picture from Valparaiso in Chile and my interpretation of the picture from that forecast differed greatly from the forecast coming through from Bracknell. It was back to a typical situation where I was struggling to work out which was the best way to go. It was difficult to convey to the crew what we were doing and why, when I wasn't really sure and the two sources of information didn't agree. Robert and Richard were working hard at the weather fax to try to get further sources of information so that we could finalise our plan.

Despite the confusion, we pulled up to second equal position. It was amazing how that improved morale. I'd predicted the right weather change at the right time – great for my confidence. At this time we'd been puzzled to see *Group 4* pass close astern of us at night going downwind in the wrong direction and it was obvious they had some kind of problem. The deck lights were on and we could see the sails at the front end flapping; we assumed that they had either torn the headsail or maybe just broken a sheet or had some form of front end problem. Later we learned on the Chat

Show that the forestay bottlescrew had broken and they were heading into the Brazilian port of Florianopolis to await a replacement.

There's nothing like something breaking on an identical boat to make you have a good look round your own. At the first opportunity, we began a thorough inspection of our own rig. Matt and I made a special check on all the fittings – we marked the positions on various rigging screws so that we would know if anything had moved. Because we didn't have any detailed information on what had happened to *Group 4*, we checked everything. Afterwards we were certain that the mast was still straight and we were quite happy about the rig.

Sunday, a week after the start, was a wet morning with lots of hard physical work on deck. We had three headsail changes and had put two reefs in the main inside three hours. That amount of work is non-stop physical effort – these were big sails so everyone was continually working, changing the sail, folding it, getting the next one ready, putting a reef in; there's no time to sit and adjust and yet you're constantly wet and tired. I had to stop myself getting too involved because of my knee. To take a sail down you have to kneel down to be able to pull it on to the deck and when I helped out that morning I twisted the knee again and gave myself another three days of pain. So I became very wary of going forward of the mast. After a rough patch, the crew seemed to be getting their sea legs – only Phil and Sam were still slightly ill at that time and Phil had only been sick once. This was good news as it indicated that we were soon going to have a fully fit, able crew.

For the last day or so we had been fighting for second place with *Commercial Union*. Now they were only about 400 yards ahead and for the next five or six days we stayed within 6–10 miles of each other. We noticed that, in 21 to 23 knots apparent breeze, they had the genoa up. We hoped that it was not doing them too much good compared to our sail plan of No. 1 yankee and staysail and one reef in the main. We were more upright and it appeared we were gradually overhauling them. We also saw that they had half their crew on the weather rail – Richard Merriweather, the new skipper, was obviously pushing it hard. It was good to see them with improved morale following that first contentious leg.

We now had our first opportunity to use our new asymmetric spinnaker in a solid breeze of 20 to 25 knots. Once hoisted it took all my strength and experience to drive the boat, and we damaged the mast fitting. The track on the front of the mast that the pole fitting attaches to was twisted and bent. We found, at the time, that the sail has so much power it is very difficult to find the right breeze and the right angle of wind to fly it successfully. On our next attempt we decided to tack it down to the deck and not use the pole. The damage shook both the boat and the crew, although I tried not to let them lose confidence in the sail. I thought that once we learned more about it we might find a useful wind range for it.

The news from the Chat Show told us that we were losing a bit more ground to *Commercial Union*, although we were still pushing the boat hard to try to make the calm weather window off Cape Horn. Other news that came through was about the Vendee Globe Singlehanded Race. Nigel Burgess was drowned in Biscay just after the start. I'd met him in 1988 in the Singlehanded Transatlantic and he had a lovely family. At least he went doing something that he cared about passionately. This news affected me deeply – the breed of singlehanders is really quite special. Maybe he did one race too many – it could have been me. An incident like that makes you think of your own future options: maybe a BOC, another race singlehanded, or do I then decide it's time to have a family? Are all these options mutually exclusive or can I have it all? Probably only if I have enough money.

We had reached the Roaring Forties. Although our introduction was in calm weather it was noticeable how the weather was getting colder and we began to plan for the cold, deep ocean conditions to come. Certain procedures on board, such as insisting that one person in each watch wore their dry suit, gave us a nominated swimmer if necessary in a man overboard situation. The iceberg watch tightened up, both on deck and standby on the radar. Every ten minutes a crew member usually checked in all directions round the yacht; in poor visibility this was increased to every five minutes. As we headed south it also got cold below decks. I changed to my serious sleeping bag and liner for the first time in an attempt (successful) to keep the toes warm. It also became apparent that the aft 'coffin berth', where I slept, had a cold condensation spot on the deck head. It was always wet, and couldn't be dried out.

Around the same time, *Rhone-Poulenc* broke a spinnaker pole with the asymmetric up in a 38 knot gust. We believed that she had lost antennae from the GPS on the top of the radar, and other bits and pieces, had a badly shaken rig and, I would expect, also a badly-shaken crew. We knew that this sail could be more than a handful. *Rhone-Poulenc* headed for the Falkland Islands to check the rig, although we couldn't work out what damage would cause them to stop sailing unless it was a broken shroud or stay. After hearing about *Rhone-Poulenc* we removed one of our antennae and checked that we could run both units from a single antenna, so that in the event of us losing the radar strut we would have a spare antenna to run the GPS system.

About twelve days out from Rio we had 600 miles to go to the first right hand corner – I called it the 'corner' as we must have all been certifiable to want to go there; in my mind, by not stating the name, I chose to ignore its reputation. We had all been a bit preoccupied with the Horn, always making reference to it in conversation and selected books such as Chichester's *Along the Clipper Way* and *Once is Enough*, by Smeeton had become compulsive reading. Both give accounts of Horn roundings ranging from the clipper ship days to more recent yachts. The sea temperature had dropped steadily since Rio, where it was 24°C, to a chilly 7°C – definitely noticeable when taking a saltwater shower.

In six days we went from wearing the odd hat at night to now being attired in thermals from head to foot. Fashion had no place on *Coopers*, just warming qualities, and some of the colour schemes – pinks and reds next to greens and purples gave an opening for further joking. The layers had built up gradually, starting with silk underwear through thin thermals, thick woolly or fleecy thermals, jacket liners to foul weather jackets. The record number of layers went to Bertie with a total of ten – we had to wake him up in plenty of time to don this costume. My favourite attire was long johns, salopettes and a superb Sub-Zero multi-fleece jacket. The jacket, made from Tactel, was impressive for its 'lack of water holding' property – it always felt warm and dry. We found that the steel of the yacht itself chilled us by rapidly conducting body heat away as we sat on it.

Some of the temperature drop was quite possibly caused by the closeness of icebergs. The first 'berg' sighting had us all on deck looking like a group of Japanese tourists, cameras all ready to take that classic shot of 'me and the iceberg.' We saw three initially and the magic of seeing your first 'berg' still lingered. I believe everyone should see an iceberg at least once in their life. There is something eerie, yet graceful and magnificent about these large lumps of ice. Wildlife sightings of whales, seals and new species of birds, especially albatross, still brought cries of delight and stampedes on deck. We were preoccupied, but I think we were ready for the waiting to be over and actually looking forward to getting to the Southern Ocean.

In practical terms, the preparations meant a few procedure changes – lots more clothing and specialist underwear, compulsory harnesses, safety checks and covers to the dorade vents. The procedures on deck became well practised, with nominated people doing particular jobs. This was not the time for everyone to dabble in each area. Matt, Geraint, Maarten and Phil were the 'sharp end boys' right at the front, closest to all the waves and therefore the wettest. Their job was to change the sails when called for by variations in wind strength and direction. This team really appreciated their Musto drysuits. A one-piece suit with sealed-in feet and soft, neoprene seals at the neck and wrists and a water-tight front zip.

The weather pattern for the next two or three days looked quite favourable and, if present conditions prevailed, we anticipated rounding the Horn on Monday. I revised all the information we had on board regarding tides, currents, local winds and conditions in a special effort to get this one right. Prior to approaching the Horn, I had chosen to go through the Straits of le Maire, inside Islas los Estados at the eastern tip of Tierra del Fuego. This would give us approximately a day to clear the land prior to our first Southern Ocean depression. It was a narrow window and we pushed the yacht quite hard to get there in time. This nasty area of sea is caused by a shallow continental shelf, the edge of which must be an impressive cliff as it drops 4000 metres over a distance of 20 miles. When the might of thousands of miles of ocean hits this cliff, the water can only go in one direction – up.

No matter how much preparation is done some small doubting thoughts remain: will I be able to cope? How frightened will I be? Which of the crew can I rely on when it's Day three in the storm? How will the boat stand up to it? I felt sure that once the Horn was rounded, the mental pressure that had built up would quickly disappear. I made a mental note to ensure that the rounding wouldn't become an anticlimax or disappointment to the crew once it was all over – maybe we just needed to ask ourselves: how many people do you know that have sailed round Cape Horn?

CHAPTER 8

Euphoria at the Horn

The day before Cape Horn, spirits were high aboard *Coopers & Lybrand*. We were in the middle of the Le Maire Straits in bright sunshine and we had the tide with us and the lightweight spinnaker up. We were doing 9 knots (11.5 over the ground). It was incredible weather to be approaching Cape Horn. We spoke to Barry Pickthall, *The Times* sailing correspondent who was stationed at Cape Horn in a hut belonging to the Chilean Navy; he was there to organise coverage and photographs of the yachts rounding the Horn. He told us that *Commercial Union* had still not reached the Cape (thank goodness) and that there was no wind there. So much for the Screaming Fifties! I looked at the weather charts again, but they were very complex and didn't seem to show breeze. I suggested trying the asymmetric spinnaker again – this caused some cockpit discussions. A lot of the crew were still very frightened of it and therefore, a bit wary about trying it again. I'd already decided that we were going to put it up, but we had the discussion first.

It was the darkest part of a very short night – only four hours of darkness. Our waiting had come to an end – we had passed Cape Horn. On 1 December 1992 at 0530 GMT the fourteen people aboard *Coopers & Lybrand* became new members of the elite band of 'Cape Horners'. This was such a special occasion – what a brilliant feeling it was! All the crew stood on deck taking photos of each other, holding a white cupboard door on which the details of the rounding were written – both date and location. It was possible to make out the silhouetted shape of the famous rock, but I doubted if any of the photos would show it. Euphoria came easily with three bottles of champagne and toasts were made to Chay

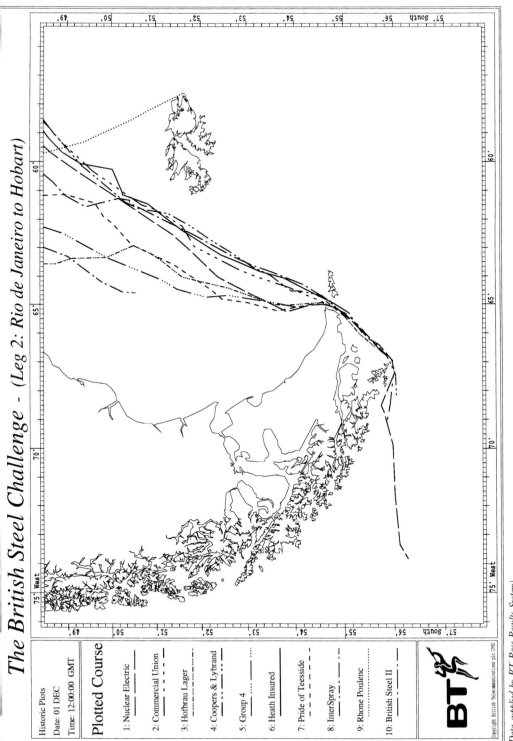

The British Steel Challenge - (Leg 2: Rio de Janeiro to Hobart)

Historic Plots
Date: 01 DEC
Time: 12:00:00 GMT

Plotted Course

1: Nuclear Electric

2: Commercial Union

3: Hofbrau Lager

4: Coopers & Lybrand

5: Group 4

6: Heath Insured

7: Pride of Teesside

8: InterSpray

9: Rhone Poulenc

10: British Steel II

Copyright British Telecommunications plc 1992

(Data supplied by BT Race Results System)

Blyth and to each other as fellow 'Cape Horners'. Homage was also paid to Neptune, with a mug of champers. This was the adventure we had all come for, the thrills and spills of ocean sailing in the notorious Southern Ocean and the conquering of the most frightening seaway in the world. A more sobering thought was for all those past sailors who didn't make it and the conditions they must have had to endure.

The conditions for us were ideal with a northwesterly breeze giving us a calm sea and good boat speed of 9 knots. The temperature had dropped further to 3°C and the boat was beginning to run with condensation, making it necessary to use the heaters. Breakfast was a real blowout celebration of sausages, fried potatoes, scrambled egg, cheese, mushrooms and other special bites. We all looked forward to the next excuse for a party – Christmas, or halfway round the world or maybe both.

Dawn was a brilliant display of natural phenomena with the orange red of the sunrise complimented by the rainbow off the port bow. The distant icy mountains and glaciers of Isla Hosta and Tierra del Fuego, reflecting all these colours, were seen so clearly that they denied their fifty miles distance. We were a bit disappointed that we had not seen the Cape clearly or in daylight and have no photographic reminders, but then some of the mystery remains for the next time. Emotionally, however, it was an amazing high.

It felt cold but we were chilled not only by the low temperature but also at the thought of our first storm. The lead yacht, *Nuclear Electric*, was two hundred miles ahead of us and battling against storm force 10 winds. With three reefs in the main and the storm staysail up, we waited for the storm to reach us. The glacial mountains of Chile were our last sight of land for what was to be 6000 miles. This was one of the great challenges, the Southern Ocean and the ultimate battle against the elements. Our plan was to stick to the shortest path as dictated by the great circle route – known in our case as the Piccadilly Line. I'd inserted and numbered all the waypoints between our current position and Hobart – Geraint had replaced the numbers with stations on the Piccadilly Line – Holborn through to Earls Court (the Australian end of town). This route took us through this awesome ocean as far from land and other people as it is possible to get, so giving names to points along the way made it appear not quite so inhospitable.

Although conditions were steady, they were affecting Phil Jones, our one-legger, who'd embarked in Rio and was suffering from seasickness. Phil was weakening and his resistance was low. In the first two weeks he'd been on deck fairly frequently, but it was now apparent that he was becoming a bit of a liability on deck and couldn't do a lot. Phil was hit all the harder by his illness because he was a keen and relatively experienced sailor and had chosen this leg specifically for the excitement and challenge it offered. However, he was still mentally fighting it and determined to keep trying.

This steady breeze ensured that we lived at a permanent angle of 30°. The simplest of tasks – even visiting the heads – took time. Once the course through the yacht from galley to forepeak had been negotiated you then had to peel off layers of clothing, praying that the helmsman would not find a big wave for the next five minutes. Afterwards, you had to make your way back knowing that one slip of hand or foot would reduce you to a bruised, sprawled heap on the cabin sole.

Sunday 6 December found us tramping along making 9 knots, believing we were having a good run and making a good course. This belief was due to a tactical decision to take a more southerly route, which would give us an advantage over the other yachts when the weather system changed. Robert who was helming, got caught by a big, unavoidable wave. As he surged down the back of the wave, with speed beginning to pick up, there was a bang followed by a repeated scream of 'The forestay has broken, the forestay has gone'. Crew below abandoned their coffee and breakfast and there was a rapid mass movement on deck followed by people struggling back into their foul weather gear while others ran straight up clad only in their thermal underwear. As we rushed to assess the situation pictures of ripped sails or broken booms flashed through our minds.

Robert was already bearing away to ease the load from the forward rigging and the foredeck crew were in action grabbing wet flogging sails to prevent any further damage. Working with bare hands on wet, cold steel at a temperature of around zero limited the time spent on the foredeck. The crew had to take it in turns to go below to warm their hands. The No. 2 yankee was taken off, stuffed down below and the loose forestay tied off. All available foresail halyards were attached to the foredeck temporarily to support the mast. As a further precaution, a third reef was put in to bring the mainsail load below the next mast support. With three reefs in, it was possible to tension both runners without interfering with the sail and therefore stabilise the bottom two-thirds of the mast.

We surveyed the damage: the bottom rigging screw – a 20 mm threaded metal bar – had sheered. The sail appeared to be intact. Neil found that two hanks had broken off. A subdued atmosphere pervaded the yacht. The two previous yachts that had suffered rigging damage, *Group 4* and *Rhone-Poulenc*, had both gone to land for assistance and initially there was a somewhat natural expectation amongst the *Coopers & Lybrand* crew that we would have to follow the same route. The thought of returning to land to effect a repair, or limping along to Hobart with no more than a staysail, filled us with dread and despondency. We didn't carry any rigging spares and were a thousand miles from the nearest land. This was the same failure that had occurred on *Group 4* at the beginning of this leg.

A brainstorming session was needed. Various options for a temporary repair were considered and all suitable spares, shackles, lines and anchor chain were assembled. We also sent off a message to Challenge HQ back in Britain informing them exactly what had happened. Consideration was given to cannibalising other rigging, namely the babystay; although it was a bit smaller, we thought it would do the job. The option of returning to land was hardly considered. It was apparent to me that we had to effect an immediate repair and then decide where we were going. I knew that if we went to Chile for repairs (the nearest point of land), Valparaiso was the only contingency port that was feasible and this was half way up the coast of Chile, not in the southern section. Once there, there was also the consideration that we would be closing an unfriendly lee shore with a damaged yacht. Also, spares flown out from England to Chile could take a considerable time to reach us.

After considering these various factors, I firmly believed that if we went back to Chile we would not catch up with the fleet and would never make it to Australia – effectively we would have been out of the race. However, we still had to make a repair before we went anywhere. Matt inspected the babystay and inner shrouds and recommended the aft lower fitting as suitable. Arnie, Bertie and Titch took it in turns to dismantle the port leeward lower (it was not loaded because we were on starboard tack) and rebuild the forestay with the bottom fork and the threaded screw. Once it was reassembled, Matt and Arnie put the tension back on the forestay. It was an extremely wet, cold job to carry out right on the bow of the yacht whilst we were still sailing, digging into these Southern Ocean waves. There were many anxious moments while the repair was being carried out – would it hold? All this time we were being escorted by two or three albatross. These great ocean birds came close to take a look before soaring away, never appearing to move their wings and totally unconcerned by these yellow blobs rushing about the vessel.

The repair to the forestay proved to be 100 per cent effective on this tack – we were amazed and delighted by this as we had not thought that it would be possible to sail on at maximum efficiency. With all the crew clear of the foredeck we set the yacht back on course. We were able to resume our track with only a 2 hour delay. We surprised the fleet at the speed of our repair, as similar damage had cost *Group 4* a two day delay. We were also very chuffed with ourselves for overcoming a mishap that had forced one of our competitors to head for land. It called for a celebration – a mid morning beer, chilled of course. The best story to come out of the whole incident concerned an off-watch crew member, John Kirk, who claimed that on realising everyone would be on deck, he rushed to the galley to see if any food had been left behind!

All the fleet had been informed of our breakage and the other skippers called up with offers of assistance and concern. Both *Heath* and *Group 4* both offered to supply parts for repairs if we needed to make a rendezvous. It was very reassuring to know that they were there and heartening to talk to them all. The true cost of our misfortune was to lose approximately 20 miles to our competitors. We managed to hold on to third place but the race was getting closer and there was still 4400 miles to go to reach Hobart. However pleased we were with our quick repair, we still had to find a suitable way of tensioning the aft lower shroud. Shortly, we were going to have to make some northing which meant tacking to port. We were already at 59° south, which tactically, was as far as we wanted to go. It was therefore very pressing that we got the aft lowers tensioned so that we could make our tack and start going in the direction we wanted. We were not convinced that the temporary aft lower shroud lash-up would hold, but until we needed to tack it could not be tested.

We tried further modifications to achieve suitable tension on this shroud. Over 20 hours we had two people working on the modifications on the port side deck. Attaching block shackles and lines in the conditions that prevailed was an acrobatic feat. Harnessed on to the leeward side or to the mast with the sidedeck awash, high levels of concentration and determination were needed as icy waves swept over crew struggling to work. Half an hour was the absolute maximum that anyone could manage before their fingers became too numb and stiff with cold to function properly; many of the crew couldn't manage that long. The power of the waves would dislodge wedged feet, knocking crew back in the scuppers so that they had to shuffle back and wedge themselves in position again to continue the work.

One of our attempted modifications involved a four to one purchase block and tackle with the line led back to a main deck winch and required the removal of a spinnaker pole. The 25 foot pole had to go down below as it was the only safe stowage place. It certainly made getting into the cabins a little bit trickier. We had reached our seventh jury rig design and were still convinced that this route of taking the rigging screw from the aft lower to the forestay was the best way to go so we persevered. However, we began to doubt our conclusions after two attempted tacks both resulted in failure. In the first tack the lashing cord between the bottlescrew and the deck clevis pin snapped and in the second, the 18 mm spectra line broke in two places. The importance of this piece of rigging was becoming more and more apparent to us – as was the side bend in the mast. Since the aft lower was the same size as the forestay it must be carrying a big load and we were fully aware of how vital it was to keep the mast straight.

Eventually, to enable us to tack safely, we dismantled the repaired forestay and returned the vital bits to the lower shroud and tacked. We went back to the drawing board or in our case, the chart table, to come up with a solution. We were not alone in exercising our grey cells. A lot of the other skippers called us on the radio offering ideas and suggestions. The problem brought us together and engendered a feeling of solidarity. Andrew Roberts, Technical

Director, winged frequent telexes to us with practical hints from the Challenge base.

Gloomy Monday took a turn for the worst when *Group 4*, who'd had the same problem two weeks ago, lost their forestay again. Six hours later a third yacht, *Hofbrau*, joined the 'forestay club'. We were going slowly – not really in the right direction – and had lost our third place to drop to a dismal sixth. By this time, I was more convinced that a jury-rigged forestay had to be a better solution. Robert, Matt and Titch and I bounced ideas around before we came up with a sound scheme. Further thought produced a sketch and plan to carry out this modification. It was now late in the evening and as we were a boat-load of tired, cold and despondent people, tomorrow would be the day to put this plan into action.

On Tuesday, the plan was set and all procedures written down in the order they needed to be carried out. To jury-rig the forestay, all the rigging tension needed to be released to allow the mast to go straight and forward; once the forestay was tied up, the mast could then be moved back again to tension it. We began at 0830, ship's time, and eventually finished $4\frac{1}{2}$ hours later. We decided to keep the deep-reefed mainsail up to make the motion more comfortable. These jobs were time-consuming enough without having to concentrate on keeping your balance. With a rolling sea we had to gybe a few times so that the load from the mainsail would alternate on each side and we could gauge how straight the mast was.

Everybody on board worked very hard for several hours to get the job done; from logging all actions, handing the parts required, helming, wielding adjustable hammers, to making the endless cups of tea, there were jobs for all. Ann reminded us of an exercise we had done at a team building weekend the previous summer. The exercise involved paper, wooden poles and planks, rope and string and the aim was to build a wind-powered machine to lift a bucket of water two metres. Perhaps it helped to sharpen our thinking and powers of problem solving. The exercise back on land had certainly been easier, as out here the stakes were higher – indeed our vessel, home and lives depended on our solution.

We still had to prove that our jury rig would hold. We believe that this latest version was our best chance at the time but we were not to know what tomorrow would bring. If we had lots of breeze we would be happy as we wouldn't need to carry any sail on the

Jury rigged forestay

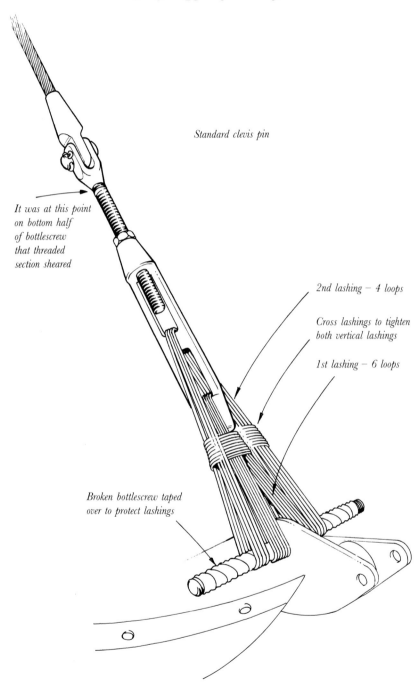

Standard clevis pin

It was at this point
on bottom half
of bottlescrew
that threaded
section sheared

2nd lashing – 4 loops

Cross lashings to tighten
both vertical lashings

1st lashing – 6 loops

Broken bottlescrew taped
over to protect lashings

Procedure for jury rigging the forestay

1 3rd reef the main.
2 Drop the staysail.
3 Helm off the wind.
4 Mark the setting of both cap shrouds. Loosen them 5 turns each.
5 Loosen backstay completely.
6 Attach forestay hardware.
7 Do Kevlar lashings.
8 Loosen inner forestay.
9 Tighten backstay until straight fore and aft.
10 Tighten babystay and lower shrouds – keep the bottom section of the mast in column. Equal number of turns on lower shrouds.
11 Tighten inner stay and backstay to keep bottom half of mast straight; 2 turns on each until correct. Check by gybing.
12 Check intermediate stays.
13 Tighten backstay (when all others are straight) to tension the forestay.
14 Tighten cap shrouds back to their setting in (4).
15 Complete visual inspection.
16 Go back on the wind and tack to each side to check tension (3rd reef only).
17 Re-mark the running backstays to show correct mast shape.

See page 98 for forward view of rig.

Forward view of rig

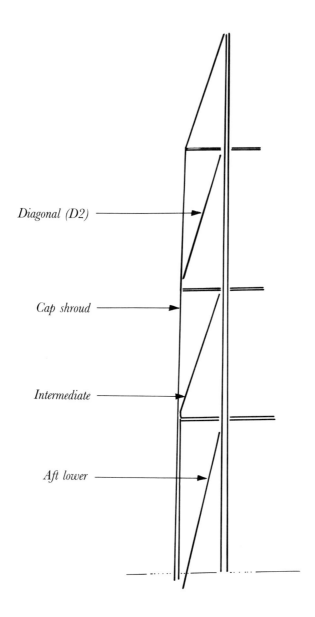

Diagonal (D2)

Cap shroud

Intermediate

Aft lower

forestay to make up the boat speed. We were still in touch with the fleet but there was another 4000 miles to go. It was the following day that we first had a sail on the repaired forestay. We hoisted the No. 2 yankee and there was no noticeable sag although the cap shrouds and the lowers still needed tightening. We again took the No. 2 yankee down to effect this adjustment, which took another three hours.

The other problem we had later that day, when we got as far as trying to put the full mainsail up, was that the mast was obviously backswept, ie more raked, and the boom was sitting on the kicker strut, so we had to shorten the kicker strut to maintain the correct sail shape. My private concern was that I knew we'd damaged the mast, it was certainly bent and there was the possibility that further damage had been done. We therefore worked very hard at keeping the mast straight and in column.

It also became apparent from below that the mast was actually moving at deck level. As long as that movement stayed within the boundaries that I had set myself, we would continue. If these boundaries had been exceeded prior to reaching the waypoint at 120° west and 52° south, then I would have turned the boat round and headed back to Chile. Those were the thoughts in my mind. Every other day we were making some adjustment to the rig. It was also coming out on the Chat Show that people were seeing icebergs around the way-point.

As I began to realise how badly the mast was damaged I resolved to keep the knowledge completely to myself. I hated the awful prospect of having to stop racing and run for Chile and the last thing I wanted was for the crew to be as worried as I was. I would sit at the chart table lining up the edge of the mast with the bar in the forepeak, squinting at it to see if it was moving more than yesterday. If it was going to break it would go either at deck level or close to the gooseneck fitting.

On the same day that we went round the waypoint, *Heath's* forestay had broken and they were in close proximity to a very large iceberg. They suffered no damage because Adrian Donovan, the skipper, had put a snap shackle release to the tack of the yankee, thus avoiding any sail damage. Having once stood admiring icebergs like Japanese tourists, our attitude towards them changed as conditions deteriorated. In a force 8 gale in thick fog, an iceberg is not something you wish to come across.

The final act of the Great Bottlescrew Saga was the news that *British Steel II* had lost her mast. The damaged bottlescrew fork that they had replaced from the forestay to the lowers went and the mast broke at gooseneck and deck level. None of it was saved. When the news came through my first comment was 'Well that should make us sixth overall'. The crew thought of me as a cold-hearted woman – am I? Perhaps it seemed that way at times, but I was a racing skipper. At least no-one was hurt but they had to assess the quantity of fuel needed to get to land. We calculated that their nearest port was approximately 1500 miles away. We offered them fuel but, as we were east of them on a similar track, it would not have been an ideal rendezvous.

Reflecting on *British Steel II's* mishap, it made me glad that I had stuck to the jury-rigged forestay, even though it appeared I was bucking the trend and acting against advice from base. I was convinced that our method was the best one, but I still had to keep justifying it to the crew. I would say to them, 'The forestay can break, but at least the rig will stay up. So we'll just jury-rig another forestay until we get there'. I was determined that we would carry on racing to Hobart.

CHAPTER 9

Trials of the Southern Ocean

Looking back at the diary entry for 15 December, I find 'WHAT A DAY, WHAT A DAY', written in stark capitals across the top of the page. It began with the worst storm that we'd so far encountered aboard *Coopers & Lybrand*. Our instruments were unstable so we couldn't precisely record all the weather data, but from information passed from the other boats and reports afterwards, it seems likely that we had wind speeds of 65 to 70 knots – force 10, gusting 11. There was so much spray flying that half the time we couldn't see the waves, but I estimate that they were perhaps 35 feet high. The crew were convinced they were 50 to 60 feet high. Phenomenal! This wasn't just hyperbole from us; the crew were delighted to find that in the official Admiralty Guide, waves of over 30 feet are listed as 'phenomenal'.

At this point we had already dropped the mainsail, as even with three reefs we were overpowered and we were sailing just under the staysail. We were already two-and-a-half crew down: Phil was completely confined to his bunk with severe seasickness, Robert was still out of action with cracked ribs having been thrown against his bunk rail much earlier on in the leg. His ribs were not making the improvement we'd hoped, but being a particularly stubborn Scotsman, Robert had been unwilling to take the role of an invalid and stay below for a while on light duties. Apart from pain killers, there was no treatment we could offer on board apart from not loading the injury, which meant avoiding winching or any physical work. Titch had also taken a fall below deck and knocked his ribcage. We didn't know whether it was simply bad bruising or worse but he was taking painkillers and finding it difficult to undertake any deck work.

I'd made a decision during the night that we were going to need the storm trysail because the bad weather looked set to last for at least another 24 hours. Having put the trysail up once in the Solent, even though it had been 30 knots and a very flat sea, we knew it was going to be a very awkward task and required assistance from nearly all the crew. We needed ten bodies to do this and daylight. The trysail was laid out ready in the companionway and stopped with rotten cotton to prevent it breaking out and flogging whilst being hoisted. I'd been planning the next day's manoeuvre and was hanging my 'foulie' jacket in the locker hoping to get a couple of hours rest before daylight and the task we had ahead when I heard the shout of 'man overboard' screamed from the deck.

That cry cut through everything. For a fraction of a second I could not move. Then, everything happened very fast. By the time I had hit the MOB button on the GPS (which gives an instant record of our exact position at the time of the incident), Matt had already gone for the engine and had got it started whilst Sam rushed to wake everyone up. This annoyed me at the time because I felt that crowds of people were the last thing we needed. I realised, later, that she had done the right thing because if Brian had been lost we would have needed all the crew on deck to search for him.

Brian had been washed through the guardrails but had managed to loop his arm round a rail so that only his legs, up to about the knees, were actually trailing in the water. He was also clipped on with his safety harness.

The watch on deck consisted of John and Titch with David helming. John and Titch physically hauled Brian back on board. We got him down below, believing that he would be fairly shocked – in actual fact he had felt quite secure with his harness tight and knowing he had a strong hold round the stanchion. The two crew on deck, John and Titch, were possibly more stunned because they had seen the big wave sweep him overboard. The absolute panic and shock that they went through was initially probably harder to cope with. Later, Brian described the wave tumbling him over completely and through the guardrail. I felt a peculiar guilt as Brian kept telling me that he hadn't dropped the exhaust caps in all the confusion.

After the man overboard incident there was a fairly fraught

atmosphere. Brian, John and Titch were still in shock and other crew members were demanding information. I had to try to calm everyone down so that the story could come out. It was a tense situation, bearing in mind that we were going to carry out a complicated sail change when it got light.

We decided to keep the MOB incident to ourselves. We knew that earlier articles by journalists had caused upset at home when they described the waves, fear and general conditions in the Southern Ocean. We reasoned that everyone was safe and we felt it would be unnecessary to spread alarm both at Challenge HQ and amongst the families of those concerned.

I had mentally gone overboard with Brian at that first call and my heart rate took about two hours to calm down. I took over Robert's watch for breakfast time and later at 0600 hours ship's time, we started to put the storm trysail up. To do so we needed three watches on deck just to get the sliders into the main track.

The first manoeuvre in the trysail operation was to man-handle the long heavy sausage up the companionway from below and out on to the deck. We set up a human chain to pass it through people's arms. The old adage of 'one hand for the boat' wouldn't work at this particular point. The crew had to sit down and wedge themselves firmly on deck, clipped on, because they needed both hands to feed this heavy, unwieldy bundle forward to the mast.

The trysail was made of very thick, twelve-ounce sailcloth; it was very new and very stiff. It had sliders just like the mainsail and needed to go up the same mast track used by the mainsail. The trickiest job belonged to the person standing on the boom feeding the trysail sliders into the gate and the track. This crew had to do the operation one-handed because their other arm was wrapped around the mast to hold on. Two or three feet below, a second person stood on the mast winch, helping to get the lead right as the sliders went up into the track. As this was going on, other crew members on the halyard had to take up at precisely the right moment. Communications were obviously vital, but even when we shouted the wind would just whip the words away.

Matt and Arnie took turns feeding in the sliders because of the sheer difficulties both of working at full stretch and being cold and tired. I think the closest comparison would be if you imagine wallpapering a ceiling, working with your hands above your head, but add to that the fact that the ladder is moving and icy water is

being thrown at you every five seconds. Arnie was a real gem –
he thrived on situations like this. He loved it rough and wild – the
bigger the waves the more he liked it. He appeared not to be
afraid of anything and was a great asset to the *Coopers* crew. His
sense of humour became more English and he took all the teasing
about being a 'Dutch boy' and an ignorant foreigner in his stride
and gave back as good as he got.

It took about an hour just to get the sliders in the track. Few
people, except those who push themselves to the limit at weight-
training, would understand the pain and the screaming muscles
after this strenuous exercise. The rotten cotton stops on the trysail
did part before it was completely hoisted and it began to break
out early, which further complicated the operation. The only
injuries occurred when Matt fell approximately six feet from the
mast; his size eleven boot kicked me in the face and he landed on
his backside. Matt's impact with the staysail car bruised his coccyx.

RIGHT ABOVE   Leaving Hobart with Mount Wellington in the background.

*BELOW   There is always work to be done at sea. Brian is stitching the
mainsail with Neil passing the needle back from inside the sail!*

Page 106

*ABOVE   Neil Skinner in the 'foulies' cupboard – the warmest place on the
boat.*

*BELOW   Winching up the mast becomes part of the everyday routine, no matter
what the weather. When wrapped up against the cold, inhospitable Southern
Ocean, identities were only completely revealed once below decks. To aid
identification on the foredeck, names (and nicknames) were printed on the back
of hoods.*

Page 107

*ABOVE   Bertie and I at the keyboard of the IBM computer. We were regularly
sending duty yacht reports back to race HQ.*

*BELOW   John Kirk carrying out rope surgery. Regular maintenance was
necessary to combat the number one enemy – chafe and wear.*

Page 108

*ABOVE   Titch (top) and Brian exposed to the elements. Crashing through
waves the size of houses was part of the daily routine on the third leg, as we
lived through three weeks of gales.*

BELOW   Reefing the main was Arnie's speciality.

I suffered the worst nosebleed of my life – blood everywhere – and my first thought was 'what would I look like with a broken nose?' Luckily, both of us just suffered severe localised bruising for the next three or four days. Matt couldn't sit down and I couldn't blow my swollen nose.

By the time the trysail was sheeted to the boom and pulling, the whole exercise had taken over $1\frac{1}{2}$ hours. We took down the storm staysail after the watch change so we had fresh crew; Neil, Geraint and Richard were on the foredeck. We hove-to and, with the staysail aback, dropped the sail to the deck. This took a long time due to damaged hanks which were worn, bent or broken. The staysail had taken a bit of a hammering and a couple of seams were coming unstitched – another job for Ann.

We were now truly battened down and going along at about 7 knots with the sea still very big and confused. No matter how you try to avoid the big waves, there is always one with your name on it. You can see it coming with the top about to break, and all you can do is shut your eyes, hold on to the wheel, shout something to warn the others and get very, very wet. After the water has washed along the deck and into the cockpit it takes another thirty seconds for it to drain away. The boat usually lands with a thud, crash and a bang which shakes the rig, finishing off with a little shake at the top; it is very like watching a dog after a swim – it shakes itself starting at its nose and finishes with its tail.

The next item on my personal agenda was to get some sleep. My last rest had been a couple of hours after dinner the previous night, some fourteen hours earlier. However, sleeping under these sea conditions was virtually impossible. Also, lying in your bunk below proved to be as dangerous as being topsides. It was as the yacht fell off one of the big waves and crash-landed that Geraint did the same from his bunk. He was in the top bunk on the windward side when the lee cloth (the section of canvas that stops people falling out) gave way. In this case, the knot on the end piece of string had come undone and Geraint was violently thrown out. He hit the upright opposite, about two feet away, before landing on the floor still in his sleeping bag. John heard the crash and was immediately extremely concerned. Geraint was obviously in pain and John thought there was a possibility of head injuries. Brian and Sam, the two medics, checked him over as best they could and made him more comfortable with extra sleeping bags and pillows around; we also put the heating on. The injury was most likely either a dislocated or broken collar bone.

I quickly sent off faxes to those boats carrying doctors asking for practical advice; three of the boats came back with a radio call within ten minutes. What a great fleet! Campbell McKenzie from *Rhone-Poulenc* was first and, after a discussion, had ascertained it was probably a collar bone injury. Eric Gustavson from *Commercial Union* said the same thing but in a different way and so did John Myer from *Hofbrau*. It was useful to have the information explained in different ways because it enabled us to make our own judgement. John had also put back a dislocated shoulder on board *Hofbrau*. First we treated the pain with moderate painkillers, then we moved Geraint to a sitting position during a tack – the tack being necessary to avoid going downwind of a large iceberg. Once finally diagnosed to be a broken collarbone, it was treated accordingly by putting it in a sling. What a day!

It was then 2 pm and I had not slept since 8 pm the previous evening. The sick list now was: Phil, who was still very weak and seasick, Geraint with his shoulder, Robert with his ribs and Titch also with his ribs (after the exercises today it was becoming apparent that he really couldn't pull or winch). John was also restricted to cockpit work as he was suffering from back pain – so we were now down to nine able-bodied people. Being reduced to nine people meant that we could no longer maintain our original watch system. We changed it to a two-watch system, with five in each watch and included myself in one watch as backup. Although we put Titch in one watch, he was unable to do much deck work. There were now four people confined down below who could do little but get rather grouchy. Everyone else worked harder to compensate and the stamina they showed was a credit to them.

We were then lying fourth, seven miles ahead of *Heath Insured* due to the fact that we were closer to the great circle route, ie further south although they were further west. I spoke to *Heath* as it was Adrian Donovan's thirty-fifth birthday that day and there was a bit of banter between the skippers. With all the troubles there was a strong 'family' feeling amongst the fleet. I think the skippers enjoyed talking to each other; there was an underlying feeling of people going through the same emotions and thoughts, together with the hope that nothing would happen to anybody in the fleet. A lot of the time I felt closer to the skippers – although competitors – than to the crew. Probably it was to do with the feeling of responsibility; the fact that it is up to the 'skip' to make the decisions.

A perfect example of the duality of this relationship between the skippers, being both colleagues and competitors, came when *British Steel II* was dismasted. *Group 4* and *Heath* arranged a rendezvous with her to transfer diesel fuel that they were able to spare. I listened intently to the radio thinking of them making this transfer – a tricky operation at the best of times in a flat sea. Although the wind was light, there was a nasty roll to the sea, so they had to be very careful not to damage the boats. I was also watching conditions and relative positions very closely. Both boats would have to claim a redress, a time allowance, for whatever time they had lost and I wanted to see how much they had lost against our position. So I came up with my own assessment of what this exercise had cost them in time and distance. Both had to adjust course and come a bit further south, but I reckoned it had cost *Group 4* about six and *Heath* about eight hours. Later, time awarded in redress was to become an issue between race officials and competitors at the Hobart stopover.

We rapidly approached the International Dateline. Every 15° change in longitude represented an hour, so to keep our life simple we added in two extra hours every five or six days. We then had a time difference from the UK of ten hours. When we crossed the Dateline we lost a date not a day, as we had already had the extra hours. It looked like it could be a year with no Christmas – a thought relished by the scrooges on board. Speaking to Richard Tudor, skipper of *British Steel II*, it seemed that boredom was the worst problem on board a yacht with no mast, so we sent them some posers as a quiz to try to keep their brain cells alive.

The quiz was delayed by the inevitable parting of the jury-rig forestay – it had managed some 2300 miles and we had expected the pin to give up. The screw pin was very bent and the threads had eaten through some of the Kevlar. On closer inspection, no further damage was done to sails. We had put a preventer stop to the bottom of the yankee, so that if the forestay did go, we could keep hold of the sail. We replaced the bent pin with a long clevis pin and lashed it all up again. Time taken from the breakage to full sailing again was five hours. This time the forestay looked tighter and the mast was certainly straight. I was still not happy with the lateral bend and twist, but unless there was a flat calm for between four or six hours there was not much we could do about it.

Phil went back on deck for two watches but was still being sick. We tried to persuade him to stick to dry food, taken little and often. That night Phil was very ill again – this time with a sore throat. The sore throat meant that he was unable to swallow anything and was just continually retching for about three or four hours. I think this was about the time that Phil hit his worst depression. Brian stayed by him, talking to him and seeing what he could do. Brian is a devout Christian and, at the time, Phil didn't believe he would see tomorrow. There really was nothing we could do for him, so Brian asked him if he could pray with him which he did. It was only after that that Phil relaxed enough to be able to sleep; thereafter he did recover a lot more during the following days. This gave Brian a great confidence boost in his beliefs and Christian faith. Brian was a very stable character – and, especially in the early days, one of my strongest supporters.

The conditions made it really impossible to race the whole time and it settled into a bit of trim here and there with everyone having a go at the helm, having a chance on the foredeck – a little of everything; I guess they were fairly happy. It was very frustrating for me at times but I resigned myself to making a major contribution in the areas of weather forecasting, tactics and navigation.

Christmas Day saw us lying fourth in the race. It was certainly a day to remember, being in the middle of the ocean, blowing a force 7, complete with snow showers. We were probably the last people to celebrate, being so close to the Dateline, but not close enough to lose 25 December – that would have been a real shame. The atmosphere got more festive as telex messages came in for everyone and we all booked calls home. The radio Chat Show around the fleet abounded with greetings for all, from all and occasionally a Christmas carol tune with their own topical words. The title of one favourite carol had been changed to 'While Sailors Watched their Rigs by Night' and ended with the new words 'Put your faith in God not Chay, no guts, no glory, no stay', a reference to Chay's rousing send off to the crews when they left Rio. It was *Group 4* that sang this over the HF. We arranged our own carol service with Brian leading, after he had beautifully written out hymn sheets with three carols all from memory; although we realised too late that a complete line was missing from 'Hark the Herald Angels Sing'.

This really began the celebrations. Brian was dressed for the occasion in a dog collar, made for him by the crew from rolled-up cardboard. He became 'Brother Brian' for the day. During all of this the wind piped up and a second reef was put into the mainsail, quickly followed by a nip of sherry all round offered by Sam. Sam and Robert were to be our chefs for the day and they took it in turns to prepare bread, stuffing (there were two varieties, one with haggis from Robert), and croquette potatoes. My contribution was the mince pies, using the sherry bottle – still half full – as a rolling pin and the top of a jam pot for a cutter. They were to be the flat variety as shaped baking trays were not part of the yacht's inventory. I must admit that the flavour was about right, but do they always ooze filling and juice all over the oven?

We made an effort to liven up the saloon with balloons, Christmas cards, the six inch tree given to us by Coopers & Lybrand in Brazil and copious use of tinfoil. Dinner was conducted in two sittings, to enable us to get the food hot enough for all. I was on the second sitting with Neil's watch; it seemed an eternity on deck as we were tormented by wonderful smells wafting up from the galley. Soup was followed by chicken with all the trimmings; I was so full that I very nearly missed the traditional pud. The party ran smoothly, aided by the boat lurching just as the brandy was being poured over the pudding. Even that small amount of alcohol went straight to most heads and the silly games started. Presents were thin on the ground, but I would really have appreciated the good old boring regulars of socks and gloves, especially the thick and warm variety! How values change – in future I promise to cherish these gifts just by remembering this very different Christmas.

We then had less than 1700 miles to go and everyone was in great spirits. It was a truly strange and memorable day and one unlikely to be repeated; it was certainly never to be forgotten.

CHAPTER 10

Boat and Knee Surgery in Hobart

The race leaders were nearly 300 miles ahead of us and would take a lot of catching. The actual order was; *Nuclear Electric*, followed by *Commercial Union* with *Hofbrau* in third place, approximately 100 miles ahead of us. We were last of the middle group with *Group 4, Heath, and Pride of Teesside* and any of these boats were likely to finish between fourth and seventh position. It was unlikely that *Interspray* or *Rhone-Poulenc* would make up much distance; There was now over 900 miles between the first and last boat.

After all the troubles of this leg, humour was still a very important ingredient to life on board. In one radio Chat Show we'd already changed the yacht name to 'Cripples and Liedown' and it was interesting that some of the existing nicknames of the crew evolved further as time passed on. We had a 'Twitchy Titch', a 'Patient Pike', 'Sleepy Sam', a 'Bear-away Bertie', a 'Deviating David' a 'Brother Brian' and a 'Manyana Maarten'.

As we began to head north the weather warmed up and spirits began to rise with the temperature. Due to TV-withdrawal symptoms, Robert's watch devised a memory game of listing all the TV programmes they could remember from the last twenty years. The game was only planned to last for one watch to keep people awake, but it actually lasted for four days with the whole crew joining in.

With an estimated week to go and still in seventh place, we steadily gained on *Group 4, Teesside* and *Heath* during the last five days. We tried to maintain this whilst making the northing, to get into fourth place. That was probably the best we could aim for on this leg. We were unlikely to catch *Hofbrau* unless they were caught in a calm, perhaps across Storm Bay.

On New Year's Eve I gave the crew a pep talk – it was intended to be a rousing, inspired speech from the skipper – whilst having a celebratory drink. The main points I put over were that there were only 1000 miles to go, and we could get a fourth place, if not better, if we pushed it. Most of the crew were in really good shape and so I encouraged them to make extra efforts. I felt confident because I had sailed in Storm Bay before and I knew the local conditions; three years earlier I had been in Tasmania to compete in the Three Peaks Race.

There was a high over the Tasman Sea and we carried a westerly breeze right at the southern edge of the high. It looked like it would hold until the high moved away eastwards, and by then we would be well west of the mid-fleet and able to secure fourth position. We heard that *Nuclear Electric* had hit a calm and had covered only 17 miles in 12 hours, so in the previous 24 hours they had gone from 400 ahead, to 299 miles ahead, which gave us more encouragement. The fleet would bunch together and our aim was to pull further away from the mid-fleet and lessen the distance to *Hofbrau*.

As we approached Hobart, Titch was involved in checking the inventory spreadsheet and looking at the course for Leg Three. He was still on light duties down below in the galley and dealing with the faxes. His ribs were obviously cracked and he was still in pain. Without him as mate I found it very difficult to get into a routine and although I kept him informed on all sailing and tactical decisions, he tended to be a bit remote and talk to the crew rather than to me. I think he was feeling isolated and fed up with galley duties. Like most of us, Titch's moods tended to swing with the wind – sometimes he was happy to make decisions and push the boat and crew along, but he could also become unresponsive and just want to be one of the crew.

It was at about this time that the message came over the Inmarsat that *Hofbrau* had a severely damaged mast with a crack at deck level. Knowing it was damaged, we carefully monitored our own mast at deck level; it hadn't been moving outside the boundaries I'd set when we'd passed the waypoint, 4000 miles back. We had a dent spanning about half the circumference of the mast at deck level which we found difficult to get a good look at. By feel we found that it had not yet opened to a crack, but was certainly moving. The tell-tale alloy stains down the mast should

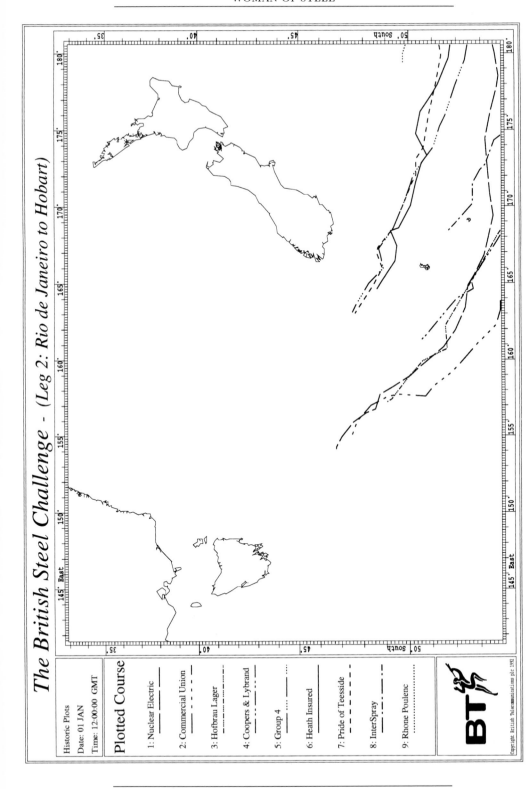

The British Steel Challenge - *(Leg 2: Rio de Janeiro to Hobart)*

Historic Plots
Date: 01 JAN
Time: 12:00:00 GMT

Plotted Course

1: Nuclear Electric

2: Commercial Union

3: Hofbrau Lager

4: Coopers & Lybrand

5: Group 4

6: Heath Insured

7: Pride of Teesside

8: InterSpray

9: Rhone Poulenc

BT

Copyright British Telecommunications plc 1992

have given us a clue, but I'd wrongly diagnosed this as just the movement in the lower kicker strut attachment. However, the mast was still up and we were making the best possible safe speed for Hobart. Worry over the problems of the last 24 hours had been more intense than any other time in the race to date.

We reduced the number of sail changes to ease the stresses on the mast and rigged extra supports to keep the lower section straight and in column. We also rigged a temporary kicker to the toe rail which gave an obstacle course when en route to the foredeck, nicknamed the 'Cats Cradle'. This was more for mental therapy but it did remove some of the compression load on the mast at the gooseneck. At that stage we felt that we had done everything we could to prevent further movement, even so every noise, creak or groan sent shivers down our spines and an uproar of large butterflies in the stomach. At each sail change – now kept to a minimum – we were acutely aware of how close we were standing to the mast. Which way would I jump? Would it give any warning prior to falling? Regular inspections were now included in the watch duties and, at that time, there was no further movement. The damage had been caused when we had the original forestay trouble. Small wonder it was difficult to keep the mast straight; still it had lasted about 4000 miles or so, so we thought that another 400 miles would be possible, especially with the extra supports.

With any troubles, there is a saying that they tend to come in threes. Other minor trials were the radar refusing to operate on a foggy night and, at the same time, the No. 2 yankee leech line snapped again, causing a worrying sail flogging noise. It was the second time that the leech line on this sail had snapped. The first time it took us nearly 20 hours of work below deck to rethread a mouse line up through the 60 foot long leech of the sail to pull through the replacement of 6 mm pre-stretched multi-braid cord. Having gained experience on that first incident, we were able to reduce the repair time, on this occasion, to 4 hours so that we could put the sail back up straight away – all credit to our sailmaker, Neil.

Sail repairs had been an item of general discussion the previous summer when Chay and the race organisers had decided that the yachts would not carry sewing machines. Most of the skippers felt that sewing machines would be fairly essential. Obviously within the Challenge ethos, unless they could get ten identical machines then no-one would carry them. They tried quite strongly to persuade us that a sewing machine was of no use for repairing the mainsail or other heavy sails, a fact which I think we were generally aware of. However, I thought that a major spinnaker repair by hand would be as easy as trimming a lawn with nail scissors!

We started to prepare for our arrival: flags, sail covers and fenders were brought out of deep stowage and an intensive clean-up was organised. The mooring lines, broken in Rio, were spliced back together and looked like a snake after a gorged meal. Replaiting this braided rope took John hours of concentrated work. He had never described himself as a handy man and working with frayed, fiddly rope ends really taxed his patience. We found that the mainsail cover had got wet and after six weeks in the forward bulkhead had sprouted all sorts of mould and fungus. Elbow grease, scrubbing brushes and bilge cleaner soon put a stop to the growth and stains, but it took continual salt water rinsing to really clean it. Like the mainsail cover, all of us felt that these last two months at sea had aged us about a year.

On 4 January we learned that the first two yachts were in port, celebrating. We had less than a day to go and had begun to dream of that first bath and beer. By all accounts, we were assured of a rousing welcome in Hobart, the noise and bustle of crowds of people was something we were actually looking forward to. After six weeks on a 67 foot yacht with the same 14 people, I guess that was not so surprising. We were still lying in fourth place and aimed to hang on to that. The last week had gone by very quickly as rapid progress had been made. It justified our decision to go south, even touching 60°, to keep the distance travelled to a minimum; so enduring the cold was worth it.

We were determined not to limp into Hobart, damaged rig or not. We had pushed the boat to the limit during the previous 4000 miles and had caught up over eight hours on *Hofbrau* as a result. However, as we hoisted the spinnaker coming up the final stretch of the Derwent River I was at last forced to admit just how badly damaged the rig really was.

My previous experience of going up the Derwent River had been extremely frustrating, with wind shifts up to 130° and wind strength variations of about 2 knots to 80 knots. We knew it was likely to be tricky but, as it happened, we came up on a broad reach across Storm Bay doing 10 to 11 knots and as we turned downwind and the breeze lightened a bit, we were still doing 7 to 8 knots. It was at this point, where it would have looked good if we could finish with the spinnaker, that I suggested this tactic to the crew. They thought it would be worth it just to see the look on Chay's face. So we got it all ready and for the last two and a half miles we flew this kite to the finishing line. I had been warned, however, that we would be unable to gybe. We had used all our spare blocks in making the extra supports around the mast, so that we would have been unable to set up the lazy guy and the sheets in time to fly the spinnaker on the other gybe.

We had such a resounding welcome, at the Elizabeth Street Pier which was lined with people four or five deep. It had been announced on the television half an hour earlier that the next yacht was due to finish and everyone came out for an evening look. It was an indication of how everybody in Hobart, and certainly Tasmania, was interested in the Challenge and all forms of sailing. The following day, the local riggers and insurance assessors were inspecting the mast. Once all the packing and foam had been removed, one was heard to remark 'How on earth did you keep that up?' The answer was probably by the prayers and mental will-power of 14 people for 4000 gruelling miles.

When the masts were finally pulled from the boats it was possible to see the damage clearly. It was perhaps more impressive to the other skippers and crews than it was to us, as we had lived with it for so long. There was a crack from the track all the way around one side and round the front – almost two thirds of the way round the mast. It also had a distinctive kink and bend in the lower half section.

The mast from *Hofbrau Lager* had suffered a very similar crack, although it hadn't been bent. *Hofbrau* had taken the boom and the mainsail off and subsequently received a lot of media attention showing how they were limping in with this severely damaged mast. By contrast, we felt that by keeping the mast steadily loaded we would get there quite safely. Having covered the last 4000 miles like that without any significant mast movement we thought that it would give us an opportunity maybe to close the distance on *Hofbrau* and so we went for it. All credit to the integrity of the repairs and the faith of the crew that we were able to sail in, appearing to be reasonably unconcerned, and with the kite flying.

I'd had continual problems with my knee since the start of the race and had been wearing the brace for most of the second leg, so the medical attention that I was due to receive in Hobart had been pre-arranged from Rio. Arriving in Hobart, events happened at speed – we arrived on the Tuesday, I saw the doctor on the Wednesday and I was in the hospital for an inspection on the Friday. As it happened, the cartilage was torn and so the damaged section was removed. I was in and out of hospital in 12 hours and on crutches for a day or so, then seeing the doctor to find out how the injury was healing. His long-term prognosis was that if I was lucky I should have a 100 per cent chance of recovery. After a few weeks of physiotherapy treatment and working in the gym, the muscles in my leg were back to full strength and there appeared to be no further problem with the knee cartilage.

The boats had travelled faster upwind than predicted and we had arrived in Hobart ten days ahead of the planned original schedule. Although it gave the crews a longer holiday, work always fills the time available and the boats had a lot of work to be done on them including slipping them for hull inspections and anti-fouling. *Pride of Teesside* knew that she had been leaking water at the skeg connection, so naturally Andrew Roberts and the technical team were anxious to inspect the hulls of all the yachts. About five of them, including *Coopers & Lybrand*, had a weld crack in the same area. Amongst other damage discovered, as the boats came out of the water, was that *Nuclear Electric*'s keel was cracked in half – it certainly looked quite impressive and from the tales we heard it must have happened whilst at anchor in Rio. The crew on board had heard a crack like a gun retort; they checked the rig and, when sailing, loaded the boat up. There was no apparent damage and it obviously didn't slow them down. The *Nuclear Electric* crew were especially horrified when the damage was revealed – particularly as John Chittenden, the skipper, had arrived in Hobart saying 'I haven't got any damage'.

I had formed my own judgment at the time on the question of redress for the yachts that had gone to the assistance of *British Steel II*. In Hobart this became an issue because the Challenge race office had made a recommendation, which then had to go to a protest hearing, of twelve hours for *Group 4* and fourteen hours to *Heath*. Competitors should be encouraged to go to another yacht's aid but I felt that those recommendations were outrageously generous. Six hours was awarded to *Teesside* who, although she had never rendezvoused, was claiming redress for having altered course. My view was that *Teesside* positively gained by adjusting her course slightly south, with the weather pattern that we had at the time. This whole issue later developed into quite heated discussions, not only between skippers, but also in the press – it was a lovely story for them.

The protest hearing upheld the Challenge's recommendation, therefore those were the time allowances given. It was very frustrating for us finishing twelve hours ahead of *Group 4* and twenty-four hours ahead of *Heath* to find that margin drastically cut down. The issue never really went away. When I looked at the methodology behind the redress used by the race office, I found that they had compared loss and gain against only one yacht in the fleet, *Interspray*. In my view, this appeared to be very unfair, as *Interspray* was on a particularly fast roll at the time (averaging 9.4 knots). It was also more than 300 miles astern of them, whereas the leading boats were a lot closer and encountering similar conditions. Extending this calculation, against the other five boats: *Nuclear Electric, Commercial Union, Hofbrau* and ourselves, as well as *Interspray* and the results backed up what my original judgment had been. The hours calculated varied from between three to ten hours for *Group 4* and between six hours and twelve hours for *Heath*. *Teesside* actually gained on three yachts.

It was our opinion that, having used that method, they should have extended it to all the other yachts in the race, to ensure that it was seen as being fair and generous. Under the IYRU Regulations, Matters of Redress, the words state that you must consider redress against 'all yachts in the race'. In that case I should have also looked at *Rhone-Poulenc* who was even further behind than *Interspray*. A generous average of all of the yachts would have been fair. It left an aftertaste that spoilt the Challenge for a while, because we felt the race was compromised, although from now on we accepted the judgment.

The dismasted *British Steel II* finally arrived in Hobart, having motored 3500 miles to reach Tasmania. The question of her reinstatement in the race became an another item of considerable discussion amongst the Challenge competitors, but my opinion was that the yacht could complete the race provided that it was seen to sail over the finish line. The rules allow for motoring to ports of refuge and a previous precedent had been set when *Rhone-Poulenc* motored 300 miles to the Falklands and received no additional penalty, just their total elapsed time. Therefore, my view and *Coopers & Lybrand's* view was that this would happen in the case of *British Steel II*. In explaining this to the crew I reasoned that *British Steel II* was so far behind the last boat into Hobart – I mean six days, probably, behind the last boat and by now, overall seven or eight behind us – that they would certainly have their work cut out if they were going to manage to win overall. If they did pull back that amount of time in two legs then they probably deserved to win it.

Ten new mainsails had arrived in Hobart and it had become a matter of concern amongst the crews that they might be issued to the yachts as replacements, whereas it had been a fundamental premise of the race that the sails you were issued with at the start were the ones that had to get you round the world. On board *Coopers & Lybrand* we had a deliberate policy of looking after our sails – hence the retaping of the mainsail seams in Rio – and felt that our mainsail was in reasonable shape. Yes, it had sailed halfway round the world and looked a bit tired, but it had very little damage, apart from a leech line problem. We had heard rumours that one or two sails were quite badly damaged and therefore felt that this would give us the advantage we had worked for on the final two legs. We didn't want this to be seen as a 'my mainsail's better than yours' scenario, but alternately we felt we had earned the right to maintain what we perceived as an advantage on the next two legs.

It was an indication of the sensitivity of the whole issue of the new mainsails that, at a time when a few people had seen them and realised they were in Hobart, their very existence was still not being acknowledged. There were inherent problems in any combination of solutions for either carrying both mainsails and accepting a penalty if you used the new one or changing all the sails at Hobart. At the end of the day we all agreed that we would stick with the existing mainsails and prove the Challenge right, that you *can* sail round the world with only one set of sails.

Leg Three:

February 1993–
March 1993

CHAPTER 11

Fanfare out of Hobart

During our time in Hobart, many of our family and friends had made the long journey to be with us. My parents had decided to make a six week trip to Australia as they had never visited the country before. Tony also flew over to see me which was a wonderful surprise. Later Rod Perry, the Cooper & Lybrand partner who had arranged the sponsorship, arrived in Hobart and used his influence to ensure that we had all the right equipment for the next leg.

On our arrival we were treated to three nights at the Sheraton Hotel which seemed unbelievably extravagant luxury after 50 days at sea. Breakfast was an elaborate buffet and I think we surprised the hotel staff by the amount we ate! After this initial treat, accommodation was spread between a holiday flat for about six people, sited ten minutes away from the harbour, and our yacht.

Tasmania was thoroughly invaded by the Challenge crews; wherever we went we met the others, even at the top of Cradle Mountain. I used this climb as a test after my knee operation; it reassured me that I would be fit enough for Leg 3. The country and its people won over hearts. It is a really beautiful island with some of the most stunning coastal scenery and headlands that I have ever seen. Wineglass Bay and Raoul Point remain indelibly printed in my mind. Tasmanians showed us a relaxed hospitality, welcoming the Challenge with open arms. Each yacht had been adopted by an assortment of yacht clubs, restaurants and other organisations. The Royal Yacht Club of Tasmania were our individual hosts and we enjoyed many evenings in their bar swapping sailing stories. Six weeks of generous Australian hospitality in a beautiful, relaxing environment, enjoying dinners, barbecues and sight-seeing trips left us feeling revitalised and ready for the next leg of the Challenge.

The Hobart stopover saw some major personnel changes in the crew of *Coopers & Lybrand*. Phil Jones, who had been so absolutely delighted to see land, was going back to Wales and his job at Port Talbot steel works and was being replaced by Mike Bass, another British Steel employee. Phil's passion for dinghies and day racing hadn't been dampened, but we were all fairly certain when he left Hobart that he wouldn't be going off-shore racing again. Despite the inevitable weakness he suffered after some 50 days of illness, it was a pleasure for all of us to see how much enjoyment he got out of the last few days racing as we closed Hobart. The other planned crew change was for Ann de Boer to fly back to England after sailing two legs with us. Her replacement was Gary Hopkins, a building surveyor and experienced dinghy sailor from London.

An unexpected change was that John Kirk was leaving us – this was due to injury. He had broken his back in an accident 15 years earlier. After recovering he had always maintained a very high level of fitness, participating in such sports as windsurfing. However, in the confines of a yacht at sea he simply wasn't able to maintain the physical fitness and strength which had supported his back and previously allowed him to ignore the injury. Due to the stamina requirements of life on board, any physical weakness is highlighted – like my own knee – as it can very quickly become a severe problem. Certainly, on the second leg he suffered quite badly with his back. On arrival in Hobart he went to see a doctor whose advice was not to carry on. I think John was relieved that the decision was being made for him, although he was really sad to leave.

John Kirk's replacement aboard was Martin Wright. He was 34, had done some sailing and as he was an ex-naval officer was rapidly nicknamed 'The Admiral'. He had left the Navy some three or four years before. I thought of an old joke aboard yachts that there are three particularly useless things on board – one is an umbrella, the second is a wheelbarrow and the third is a naval officer. We had never met him before, and had no idea whether he would fit in. It was certainly comforting to know that he was someone with sailing experience and from his naval training and discipline, he would at least be used to life at sea.

Although most of the crew had by now sailed about 14,000 miles and they were strong and competent, after six weeks ashore in Hobart quite a lot could be forgotten. We also had three people joining us – two who had not been aboard for at least four months and one who had never been on board one of these boats before. So we went out for a four hour training sail up and down the Derwent River. We did a few tacks and gybes, we put the spinnaker up in quite a breeze and got it down in one piece. I think everybody realised they were a bit rusty and the practice worked wonders in sharpening up their reactions and attitude remembering that, in a day and a half, we would be on the start line ready to do it all again.

On the start line one of my first thoughts was 'Who said sailing is not a spectators sport?' There were spectator boats everywhere, some of them moving in close enough to get shouted at. The old tensions and nervousness that you get at any start were back, but for once I was starting a leg of a race without a cold. *Coopers & Lybrand* was second or third off the line and we then went into a tight tacking duel down the Derwent River. It kept everyone busy and helped to remind us all what hard work it was. The weeks in port had taken their toll – weight had been put on and fitness had gone somewhere else in a true appreciation of the hospitality in Hobart. With not enough time for practice, a few careless mistakes were made on the tacks and with the sail changes.

The first night was very dark and it was quite windy. We were within a mile of *Commercial Union* and at about 11 pm we realised that they had some problems. They must have either broken a guy or ripped their spinnaker so, rubbing our hands with glee with the anticipation that this would slow them down, we continued. Ten minutes later the same thing happened to us. The spinnaker had ripped all the way down one leech tape, across the clew and most of the way along the foot tape.

All the 'new boys' fitted into the social fabric fairly quickly but there were still sailing skills to be learnt. Having already suggested to the watch leaders that they should not let the newcomers helm until they got the hang of the yacht, especially with a quartering, sharp sea, 10 or 11 knots boat speed and up to 30 knots of true breeze. However, I couldn't have made myself clear enough. Unfortunately it was Martin who was at the helm when the spinnaker blew and he was asking questions like, 'What have I done wrong? Why did it happen?' At the time I was furious because I felt it was something we shouldn't have let happen.

The *Coopers* 'Sewing Circle' went into action. The repair consisted of unpicking and then stitching in the tapes by folding over the edge of the spinnaker cloth into the open tape, sticking it with a spray-on adhesive and then zigzag stitching by hand. The problem was boredom – after the initial novelty of repairing the spinnaker by hand, it became more and more difficult to encourage people to sit there and do a fair share of stitching. Neil and Sam became our champion stitchers with sore fingers to show for it. With 75 feet to sew at a rate of 2 feet an hour it would take two or three days to finish. As it turned out it took a lot longer as we had to double-stitch the seams.

We discovered that one genoa halyard was looking very worn at the wire-to-rope splice, so we took it out of the mast, left a mouse in for re-leading it and Brian and Martin remade the wire-to-tail splice. The basic instruction for the splice came out of a rigging book but as neither of them had really done it before, I was acting as overseer and foreman. Between the three of us we managed an excellent first-time effort.

After a couple of days at sea, Arnie asked Robert to cut his hair. Arnie decided that the haircut wasn't short enough and so he shaved his head completely. It then looked a suitable style for a Buddhist monk – all he needed was an orange sheet and sandals. A few days later he said 'This is easy, I can wash my hair with just one babywipe'.

I realised that I had lost ground on helm and sail trim discipline – not a lot of trimming was being done unless they were continually reminded. We were on a power reach and both Matt and Titch were very good at getting the rest of the watch to look at the trim. On one occasion no-one would take over helming from me after nearly two hours. Few of the crew had the feel back yet, so it was a return to the old routine of sitting with them and talking them through helming the boat.

On the fifth day at sea, *Hofbrau* was in sight. It proved an excellent opportunity to build morale and confidence in trim and racing which is just as important as getting tactics, course and weather right. After a chat with Matt, we monitored their relative position, and distance during the next day to compare our boat speed to theirs to see if we were gaining or losing. We began to re-emphasise the importance of the waypoint closing velocity which is indicated on the GPS. Boat speed is all very well, but it has to be in the right direction and this figure gave us the calculated speed to Cape Town. We also set targets for the on-watch team, particularly the helmsman, depending on the conditions. In those headwinds of 30–34 knots they had to aim for boat speed of 8.8 knots or better, with a velocity made good of 5.5 to 6.0 knots. It was good to set targets because it gave a focus for attention.

Initially, we had quite light weather on this leg, but after nearly a week at sea, seasickness was beginning to affect one or two of the crew. Robert was sick for the second time and Brian was a bit ill. Gary seemed to be under par and I found that he had been taking two Stugeron three times a day! I was very surprised at this and suggested that he eased off. No wonder he looked a bit spaced out.

We now maintained a boat performance log. Matt, who had a degree in electronic engineering, wrote computer programmes which would produce polar performance graphs for the boat to enable us to know the optimum time to change sail and the ideal speeds we should be aiming for. Matt really wanted to do well and was becoming one of the stronger racing sailors on board. I'm sure he will go on to do a lot more sailing, particularly racing, and I wouldn't be surprised if he ends up crewing on a Whitbread boat or something similar.

Matt had suggested a scheme of having a core of racing people, one of whom would always be on deck and responsible for pushing the boat to its maximum. We investigated the possibilities to see how this could be done on a rota, while we were at sea for the next 25–30 days. I was concerned about the effect this scheme would have on some of the existing watch leaders. They might have felt that they were having responsibility taken away from them which would not have been beneficial either on the personal side or in helping the boat overall. We looked at the keener racers or competitive people. Obviously there were Matt and myself and four or five of the others, but it would have been difficult to develop that scheme into a workable one because some had talents in one direction, but did not necessarily have an overall boat awareness. I wasn't sure that the crew would respond to upping the pressure and drive on the boat towards racing, and was worried about dividing our established team. The whole question of whether this scheme could be implemented without dividing the crew was postponed, rather than resolved, by the arrival of bad weather.

The coffin berth (Bertie's bunk) in the aft starboard cabin became wet again and it couldn't be due to condensation as the weather was not yet cold enough. We definitely had a leak – possibly from the hatch or the cage in front of the wheel. Both proved difficult to inspect until we hit a calm patch. We changed the watches about and swapped Bertie and Arnie so that Brian and Bertie – both in the aft cabin – could 'hot bunk'. Brian and Robert both went down again with seasickness and with Gary causing some concern I worried that we would have another 'Phil' situation – which was agony to live through for both him and us. A week into the leg and we had been mainly reaching, making excellent speed. We set the GPS to calculate our ETA from our present speed of 9 knots, which gave us an ETA of 11 March. As we were unlikely to maintain this speed we reset the GPS to 6.4 knots which estimated our arrival at the Cape of Good Hope on March 20 – a lot more realistic!

There was now a front approaching, with a big high pressure behind it which appeared very low in latitude for this area. It meant a lot of westerly breeze – probably our first gales of this leg. I tried to set limits for tacking to give us preferential tacks and looked at weather boundaries in terms of latitude so that we could aim to maximise our course and speed. We caught a glimpse of *Hofbrau* about five miles astern; this was a satisfying sight – now all we needed to do was maintain it, and not make any mistakes, to come in third or fourth.

CHAPTER 12

Southern Ocean Storms

We suddenly had a spate of little things going wrong – the leech line in the No. 2 yankee broke (again) after being laboriously replaced in Hobart. It took us 45 minutes to pull through a new one whilst hove-to. This enabled us to stretch the sail out on deck and do the job as quickly as possible. On the previous leg, we had done the same operation below decks and it had taken many hours, so experience led us to change tactics. Even hove-to we made some miles in the right direction, albeit very slowly.

We'd just started sailing again when the staysail car shattered and the staysail began flogging wildly, necessitating another tack to replace the car before getting back on course. It wasn't the first staysail car to blow and we had begun to work out why we thought they were falling apart. It seemed that the lead angle from the staysail to the car imparted a bit of twist – more than the movement in the car block could cope with. We had no spare staysail cars so we moved a spare genoa car on to the staysail track. Having made this move, we also removed the last staysail car and replaced it with the last spare genoa car. Shortly after this, the staysail sheet parted. Our initial thoughts were that another car had blown to pieces. A rapid tack was made and the sheet was replaced – fast decisive actions that were a credit to all on deck.

Getting *Coopers & Lybrand* back on course was not so easy as in this part of the world we experienced about 50° magnetic variation due to the proximity of the magnetic South Pole. As a result, we could be steering a course of due north by the compass, but actually be travelling in a more westerly direction, causing some confusion for the helmsman. This closeness to the Pole also caused excessive compass deviation; the error in the compass due to its siting in the boat and proximity to lumps of iron. As I understand it, the parts made from soft iron, such as the keel and engine, are induced with a magnetic field causing the compass to give a misleading direction. Thank goodness for the GPS which isn't subject to such magnetic vagaries.

In this location, magnetic variation alters very quickly. In four days it went from 12° westerly variation to 50°. The compass becomes just a gauge or a dial to give you a steady direction to steer; you can't relate it to the actual course or direction you are travelling in – that comes from the GPS. The normal result after tacking the boat through an angle of about 100°, didn't happen. From steering a compass course of, say, 335° on starboard tack, we tacked on to port and the compass reading would be 350°. This also indicated that the induced magnetic effect had what they call a 'heel error'; depending on which tack you were on, the compass deviation varied wildly. To check on the accuracy of the GPS we blew the dust off the sextant to measure the sun's altitude – not an easy task on a pitching, rolling yacht. Using two sets of sights Martin, our new recruit and ex-naval officer, calculated our position. Then, with a second position calculated, we were able to check on the actual direction that we had travelled. This sequence of calculations would be essential if the GPS developed a fault. On cross checking our results with the GPS, our calculated position was within five miles – a pretty good estimate when there's nothing around you but hundreds of miles of ocean.

A storm approached and we were on the wind with the breeze building all day, sail reduced to the third reef and staysail. Supper ended up all over the galley floor with Sam's contact lens somewhere in the middle of it – a brief search was carried out but quickly abandoned. As the depression systems approached the wind was northerly to north westerly, which forced us to go on a more southerly tack. I tended to bias the tacking angles to encourage us to keep the northern side of the track because I still believed this would give us our best chance of making a break. We scribbled notes in the log book to work out our tacking criteria. For example we tacked on to port when the course over the ground (COG) equalled the bearing less 50° and tacked back on to starboard when the COG was 60° greater than the bearing. At this time, *Group 4* was moving like an express train. At every Chat Show

Group 4 appear to be gaining six to ten miles on the rest of the fleet.

During the previous three days our own sailing performance has been suffering. We constantly checked the sail trim, inspected the rig for movement and generally tweaked everything in sight. We even started looking for other reasons for slowness, including the helm's ability and weight distribution. I decided to check on the watertight bulkhead for ingress of water. This thought was triggered by the fact that other yachts were losing not only their masthead navigation lights, but their deck navigation lights too. This concerned me, and the one possible link that I could think of was that all our pulpits had been removed and replaced in Hobart. As I wasn't present when it was replaced, I wanted it checked. It was a good thing as lots of water came out – the drain tap poured for thirty minutes. There was obviously a leak either at the pulpit fittings or where the cables came through from the navigation lights. Three tons of water in the watertight compartment is definitely not an aid to racing trim. An hour of draining and continuous pumping solved the problem for the short term. Now this area was checked daily and we were extra vigilant when pumping out the bilges.

Group 4, was still way out in the lead. The fleet was closely bunched with eight boats within approximately thirty miles of one another. We were lying eighth. At the back of the fleet *Interspray* was still trying to catch up, having had to do a penalty leg out of Hobart because she had a new sail.

Deficient vision proved to be another problem on board. I am very shortsighted and have a choice between wearing glasses or contact lenses. I prefer to wear the specs which are in robust plastic frames (I found that metal frames corrode very quickly) and save the contact lenses for port. My main reason is that salt gets on the face and you tend to rub it into your eyes which makes them very sore. The specs give added protection against the flying water, but I found myself constantly cleaning them. Also, with irregular sleeping times – a maximum of four hours on and four hours off – taking contact lenses in and out on a boat is really quite dangerous and the risk of losing one is very high. Various combinations are used by others on board: four of us are partially-sighted. Both Bertie and Baldrick tend to use lenses during the daytime, and on watch, and wear glasses at night. Sam persevered with lenses until she lost one. Later, she also lost a lens from her glasses, which are set in thin metal frames, but luckily we found it and were able to fix them.

Titch was standing in on watch for Gary who had sickness and stomach ache. In discussions with Bertie, regarding boat performance, he suggested Matt as mate for the final leg. This idea had crossed my mind for leg four, because Matt was the most race motivated and his enthusiasm was infectious. However, Titch's organisational skills and greater sailing and safety awareness still made him the best choice for mate. I didn't want to upset Titch or the others. I kept wondering if there was another way to slip one person into a watch to rotate the changes, including the 'race people' to maintain motivation. There seemed to be no definite answers to this but we needed to keep trying. Everyone on board seemed a lot happier and more settled, compared to the last leg. Obviously they were more experienced and competent but possibly the change of personnel helped.

We now experienced the weather we had all expected from the Southern Ocean – depression after depression, following through with little or no respite between; there were gales on the nose most of the time. A steady 40 knots of wind replaced 35 knots as the typical sailing breeze. It was also very dark, very cold and the wind chill factor at 40 knots and air temperature at 4°C must have taken the temperature down to about − 30°C, although it was something we couldn't measure. Later on a weather system topped even these wind speeds by blowing up to 60 knots.

At this time we had a saga of steering faults. The wheel's spindle locking pin sheared and the wheel started pulling out from the pedestal. With the emergency tiller in place, I wedged my back against the radar strut and my feet against the aft winch. Wrapping my arms around the tiller I steered by rocking my upper body. My stint of 2 hours steering a 67 foot yacht with an emergency tiller is certainly an experience I would not want to repeat. Only a few hours earlier, we'd had our first steering failure when the collars that fitted between the quadrant and the square rudder stock had worked out so that the wheel no longer turned the rudder. I advised the crew to leave it alone thinking that the boat would settle and probably heave-to. I was amazed when the yacht kept sailing on. She was obviously very well balanced and the trim was right, so for the hour it took us to replace the quadrant and retighten all the steering cables, the boat carried on sailing at between 7.5 and 8.0 knots in the right direction with no-one at the wheel. There were a lot of jokes about not needing helmsmen. It also proved a point to the crew that sometimes if you allow the boat to follow a natural course through the waves it is better than forcing it.

The constant gales gave the crew and yacht a terrible battering. Windpowered spray viciously stung any unprotected skin and the crashing waves continually scrubbed the decks clean then washed out the cockpit. After each impact the boat recovered, shook itself, picked up speed and surged forward, and we knew that with the next wave the cycle would start again. The crew on deck were unrecognisable with faces hidden behind hats, hoods, scarves and goggles. Only in the doghouse did they emerge, red faces glowing with excitement and fear to tell of the last enormous wave. The maximum gusts of 65 knots had us holding on tight. The helmsman, with eyes shut, waited for the gust to end – the lulls at only 45 knots were a gentle respite and seemed almost enjoyable sailing. How relative values have changed – never before had I said that sailing in 45 knots of wind was enjoyable. What madness was this?

The waves found more and more novel ways of outwitting the helm – there was the straight-on 'biggy' that had no back to it. The yacht was first airborne then crashed bellyflop style. Then there were the mountain-climbing ones – a big one concealing an even bigger one behind. Unlucky the driver when these waves coincided and the top broke over us. With each of these waves the helmsmen either shut their eyes to avoid the smarting spray or ducked behind the wheel, knowing full well that the motion would whip the wheel out of your hands if you hadn't let go first. The cockpit acrobatics team comprised Matt, Sam, David, Bertie, Arnie and myself, all sporting a variety of swellings and bruises. Our showpiece was the inverted wheel spin – a very stylish manoeuvre, but the landings still required practice. Titch, on his way forward to check the sail trim, was caught by a wave that swept him back into the primary winch and then on to Geraint's lap in the cockpit. Nothing was broken but Titch was very stunned and shocked. However, after sleep and some painkillers he was fine. He stayed off deck for a day and did the cooking and tidied up the galley. Although beaten and bruised, he was then back on deck fully functioning.

Waves were given names such as 'smoker soaker', 'crapper flapper', 'stern whip' and the 'corkscrew'. Brian's pet wave-hate was the 'galley growler'. On one occasion he needed three attempts to make dinner. The first two attempts ended with chili con carne liberally distributed throughout the galley. He finally succeeded after roping the lids to the pans and the pans to the hob! There was also the 'bunk bouncer' when your nose was pressed against the headlining above your bunk or, in Baldrick's case, throwing you on the floor. Whilst Pike was helming, the boat fell off a huge wave with such force that the radio-cassette player shot off its mountings and nearly felled 'The Admiral', whizzing past his ear. Everything became wet – sodden sailors dripped in the doghouse, the washing up water leapt round the galley, the hatches leaked and water poured through the mast gate. If there was the smallest opening, the ocean found it.

Only Gary was still sick at this stage, but he did manage two hours on deck so we thought he could be on the mend. We tried a slight bullying technique: first, a Scopoderm patch, then a routine of getting him up for two hours both morning and afternoon, only feeding him 'gentle food' with no orange squash as anything acidic affects the stomach and throat. For the first time in three or four days he actually sat on the step. I decided we could not risk another 'Phil' situation and unless he showed improvement during the next five to ten days, I would not take him on the last leg. He must have had doubts himself by then as to whether or not to continue. Gary finally came to the conclusion that, although it was an experience to do this leg, he wasn't enjoying it and therefore would not want to carry on. He would then have additional time and funds back at home to get a new job and carry on with his normal life.

The Inmarsat telex system was excellent for communication, but I was already concerned that the costs incurred by either individuals or companies in sending messages would be very high. We knew that it cost about one penny per character because a newsletter going back to Coopers & Lybrand of 5000 characters long cost £50 – expensive if individuals were sending a lot of messages. It was less expensive to use the radio to link into a phone call home. That cost about £4 a minute, so we used to try to restrict the calls to 4 to 5 minutes; at least that remained manageable. Talking to people back home was always a good boost for the crew and they liked to do it on a regular basis, say once a week, or when we could get a clear line through a radio station. During the early part of the race I think the crew thought I was being deliberately awkward in limiting the access and time to both these methods of communication, but as the race continued and people back home received phone bills or bills for sending telexes they began to realise the true cost and started to limit themselves.

One of the few bits of news that we avidly sought from the UK were the latest rugby scores. Scotland had lost to England and Wales had lost to Ireland, which left scope for upsetting people both on board and within the fleet.

Titch's slight tendency to hyperactivity on board, especially with his responsibility as mate, produced a superb tease created by our new crew member Martin drawing on his naval background. Where any military unit is labelled in a condition of readiness it is colour-coded; Martin and Matt came up with 'Op Cond T' which stood for Operation Condition Tichener which then became known as the 'Twitch Factor'. The three colour codes were white, yellow and red – the white was usually shown when Paul was asleep, the yellow when he was around eating or reading, and the red was displayed whenever he was on watch. This carried on for a couple of days before Titch, joining in, started changing the cards himself. The level of teasing showed that the crew had settled back into the routine.

On 1 March we were half way through the leg. We had great reaching conditions with amazing cloud lines coming through, followed by squall lines with a few flurries of snow, although it wasn't too cold. It was good to see that the race attitude was developing with bets between watch members. Sam bet Arnie her hat against his sleeping bag that he wouldn't hit 11 knots, so he did. Sam duly gave up her hat and was then seen wearing another. We had made enough northing to happily pass the Kerguelen Islands without losing distance. Although we were still lying seventh, the middle group were very close together; there were only 60 or 80 miles separating them. *Interspray* were suffering because they had to make a lot of northing, which was costing them some distance. *Pride of Teesside* were complaining of lack of boat performance; their skeg problem had reappeared and they were letting in a fair amount of water – three or four gallons an hour was their estimate – so they were always pumping.

A couple of days later, we had a respite from the weather; the full main was up with the flattener in. We kept the flattener in as the leech was so stretched that any shape was difficult to control. The boat felt so underpowered when not fighting against lots of weather helm and a big sea that the tendency was to be oversheeted and try to sail too high. At this time, the next depression system was already making itself felt and, by inspection of the latest weather fax, there were another two depressions coming up behind this one in fast succession.

During a change from one reef to full main, Matt noticed a tear in the mainsail. There were in fact two very neat tears, approximately 16 inches long – more like cuts. We knew it had only happened within the last hour or so when the first reef had been put in. On inspection, we found there was a loose rivet on the boom and it was the raised edge, I believe, which did the damage when the main was flogging as that first reef had been pulled in. I stitched the tears with a herringbone stitch to hold the edges together, and we then made one or two patches to go over the complete area. Neil organised the patches and pre-drilled the holes so that we could do it in situ, as we did not want to take the main off to effect this repair down below. Eventually, two patches were put on, one stitched and one stuck with sticky-backed Dacron. It was a very neat repair.

The speed and intensity of the depressions showed on the barometer which, at one stage, dropped eight millibars in two hours. Our mileage covered in 12 hours was always so similar to the other boats that we wondered what we could do to gain that extra mile or two. A calm spell between the depressions reminded us that with little wind, we must keep the boat moving, so we revived the rule that the boat speed must try to hit half the true wind speed. It wasn't long before the depressions were rolling through again and it was time to be on deck and change the staysail for the storm staysail and tack.

We hove-to to make the change and Mike Bass, our new single-legger from British Steel, lost his temper when the clew fitting caught his chin as it went down below. I called him back to the cockpit and had a discussion with him regarding this burst of uncontrolled anger, which had been a danger to the other four people on the foredeck. Anger makes you go blind and deaf, although the adrenalin keeps flowing giving lots of strength. It must be controlled, otherwise it can possibly harm other people on the boat. Once I was helming and caught a gust which threw me at the wheel; the wheel spokes caught the top of my kneecap, which was very painful. Being very angry and then frustrated at myself, I stayed on the wheel for twenty minutes until my mood had abated. It was my bad knee, but it turned out to be nothing serious, just very bruised.

The consistently bad weather had its impact on us – we were all getting very tired and mood swings came and went quite quickly. On waking up to go on watch people had to be told things two or three times to make them really understand. Tolerance levels were noticeably reduced and on occasion some of the crew annoyed me. Robert became more cheerful after his birthday, but I thought he'd had enough of the sailing and it was a case of: 'I've been there and done it and I really don't want to repeat it'. He felt that this leg was taking forever and was wet, cold and tired. I also think his five days of seasickness was a worrying factor at the beginning of this leg. Sammy was also struggling; she felt that there was an overprotective attitude towards her which showed when she was not allowed to helm at times. I think it was a communication hiccup, as previously she had been less enthusiastic about helming and when the weather got rough they thought she didn't want to drive at all. This affected her so much that she felt that she had to prove her own abilities each time on every watch to different people. Sam actually does have a feel for helming but, being quite small, doesn't always have the strength to do it for long.

By now, because I would have expected that the crew would have known their own and each others' abilities a lot better, I found it curious that they didn't always pick this up – was I expecting too much from people or do I just think in a different way? I was also surprised that the desire to learn about the weather had not developed more amongst the crew. I wonder if this is a social reflection that many people nowadays expect to be taught rather than self-teach.

Titch had instigated the use of one of the port heads as a store room before the start in Southampton. With eight days to go to Cape Town he came up with the idea that we could use both heads for their designed purpose and move the stores and inventory out to some of the now empty red boxes that used to have food in them. Although it was a necessary job because everything in the stores was very wet, I think he wanted to go back to having two available heads – perhaps he was beginning to feel deprived of creature comforts and the proximity of Cape Town brought it all to mind.

The crew were getting careless regarding the boring jobs – pumping the bilges, making sure there was fuel in the day tanks and emptying the waste tanks – no matter how often they were reminded. The mate should ensure the smooth running of the onboard duties and but I don't think Titch was now committed enough – he didn't appear to enjoy the responsibility. Some people on board were naturally busy; Brian, Mike, Titch and Neil – they just get on with things in their own way. Mike, for instance, did a good job of curing a problem on the watermaker. For some reason the watermaker was not priming on the inlet low pressure side, and after taking the priming pump apart to check there was no blockage in the filters, we decided to lower the filters against the bulkhead in the 'foulie' locker. This certainly solved the problem.

It was in the last 60 knot storm that *Hofbrau* and *Nuclear Electric*, both further south, got more of a lift and made a break to get away from the pack. After we had been through a series of depressions, we were in a calmer patch and having repaired the kite we managed to repack it. We put it up and it lasted eight and a quarter hours. Robert had been having some fun driving and topped the speed we'd been hitting, which was about 12.5 knots, when he handed the helm over. It was unfortunate that the kite then blew apart with the new driver. The cloth must have been getting soft and weakening because the damage was very similar to the last time, although the tear was in a different place. At that time, being relatively close to Cape Town, we just threw the bits in a bag and forgot about it.

The weather was changing and strange things were happening. It was very difficult to predict what the wind would do – you could go from 20 to 30 knots in one direction, followed by a large wind shift to light airs in the other direction. It was an indication that we were certainly closing land, and the main weather pattern that was beginning to affect us was a high, joining and parting around the southern tip of Africa. I wanted to stay north to try to get across this belt at the right time. We were in very light weather, the middle of a high, and it was very frustrating, but we had to keep trying harder.

At the Chat Show we found we'd travelled thirty miles in the last twelve hours, although ten of those had been in the last two hours. All the middle-ranked boats in the bunch were also suffering; *British Steel II* and *Commercial Union* had only done nine miles actual distance travelled, although in both cases no distance towards Cape Town. Without the heavyweight spinnaker, we were pushing the lightweight one slightly further than we would normally do. The range for this kite is about 10 knots apparent and 18 knots true. We were already at between 12 and 13 knots apparent so we were probably pushing it too hard. We decided to change to the asymmetric, but halfway through preparing it put up the No. 1 yankee and staysail instead. We knew the wind would go further ahead, but the timescale was difficult to predict. Although it was seen as a change of mind on my part, the weather shift came through slightly quicker than we expected, hence it saved us an extra sail change and probably gave us a few more miles.

At the next Chat Show we expected the other boats to have picked up this breeze as well, and were amazed to learn that we'd made the break and were now eighty miles ahead of the boat in fifth position. *Group 4*, at this time, was closing Cape Town and only had about 100 miles to go. We also started to pick up some current which I felt would also help to keep us ahead. The wind was still fluky and the pilot books seemed to indicate that the currents should be strongest around the 200 metre line. As we were going across the current and still making a touch more northing towards the coast, it appeared that the current was then lessening; I expressed an interest in tacking in order to stay in maximum current. One of the crew who had also read the pilot books voiced a doubt about not following printed advice. We did actually do a tack for a couple of hours and I wished I'd held it longer.

It later proved that *Heath* who were further north had lost out to us, although *Rhone-Poulenc*, being slightly further south and therefore in more current were gaining. It was still a tight race and any error at this stage would lose us fourth position. Our nearness to land was confirmed when we saw our first man-made items – some gas platforms and the lights of trawlers. The birdlife changed and we were seeing Cape cormorants and yellow billed albatrosses; since there were fish jumping we were obviously over a bank. After the last calm couple of days we were actually having to wash the deck for the first time on this trip as there were no large waves doing the job for us. More rigs and ships were spotted and an aeroplane which turned out to be a coastguard came and dipped his wings as if to say 'hello' and 'welcome'.

The last night at sea was nerve-wracking. The ETA was going back all the time – we covered just seventeen miles in five hours. Our ETA became midnight on Saturday, and the only consolation was that those behind us would have less breeze and have to sail through the same fickle patch. Everyone was so looking forward to getting in that the time passed very slowly; jobs were not done, yet people said they were bored. We had to keep the boat moving just another 2 knots of breeze would have improved our trimming immeasurably. Another name for the Cape of Good Hope is the 'Cape of Storms'. What irony having 4 knots of breeze! We had been round the two most notorious capes in the world and felt quite nonchalant.

The first yacht to be spotted which called us up on the VHF was the old *Voortreeker II*, a boat I remember meeting back in 1985 with John Martin who did the single-handed BOC race in 1986. It was a reminder of what my own thoughts and aims would be after this race finished. Racing on my own again looked more and more attractive.

Leg Four:

April 1993–
May 1993

CHAPTER 13

The Final Push

The day of our arrival in Cape Town dawned with very light wind, so we knew we would be crossing the finish line at dark. Jessica Mann of Coopers & Lybrand had organised a boat to come out early and meet us somewhere off Hout Bay, ten miles south of Cape Town and take film and photographs. A Hollywood director couldn't have done a better job. We had the lightweight Coopers & Lybrand spinnaker up and were doing about 7 to 8 knots in a gentle breeze, with lovely flat water. Table Mountain came into view with a glorious sunset following it – a tailormade photo opportunity. We hoisted the yankee and dropped the kite for the TV cameras – the boat really picked up her skirts and the crew performed brilliantly. We were rewarded with a five minute news item used by the Cape Town television station on the following Saturday morning – it was all about the race, but specifically featuring *Coopers & Lybrand*.

We crossed the finish line at six minutes past nine in the evening and followed the lead boat into the harbour amid huge volumes of noise. Champagne, beer and cigarettes poured aboard. Going into the dock the inevitable confusion occurred. On the final approach towards a berth next to *Nuclear Electric*, Chay was standing on the dockside shouting 'Come in alongside'. So we backed off and came in next to Chay and the welcome really began. We had finished leg two in fourth position, so another fourth place really gave us a very consistent performance in the Southern Ocean sector of the race. It was good to see a different boat, *Group 4*, win a leg. There had been three separate winners for each leg; the only two boats that we hadn't beaten at some time or another were still *Nuclear Electric* and *Hofbrau*, who were being even more consistent than we were. The third leg had been very different because of continuing high winds, bang on the nose. The boats were pushed probably harder than any boats had ever been pushed in an ocean race which was a credit both to the yachts, crew and the Challenge shore team.

The crew were proud of themselves and quite rightly so. We had come through some of the really tough stuff and enjoyed it a lot more than the previous leg. The level of competence had really increased and confidence was 'sky high'; tasks were being performed smoothly and becoming routine. It had been quite an ordeal and, by sheer hard work, had achieved a good position.

Now this leg was over, we were looking forward to a bit of shoreside entertainment. Oddly enough, not all the crew were totally pleased to be ashore. Some of them thoroughly enjoyed the rough stuff – Matt thought the third leg was full of excitement. It was noticeable that Robert didn't enjoy being cold and wet, but when we got a good blow from behind and the boat was surging at 17 knots, he was in his element – he liked helming in lots of wind.

Poor Gary had experienced a very tough time. He had endured seasickness through this leg with gradually declining levels of tolerance and sympathy; it put a strain on everyone else being short-handed on a race like this. Gary made the reluctant decision that he wasn't going to carry on past Cape Town and do the final leg. In a sense, it was a slightly pressured choice as I asked him to think carefully about it. I felt I simply couldn't take the risk of carrying someone who was likely to be very sick again. It was not fair on the rest of the crew.

Many more families came out to Cape Town than had come to the previous two stopovers. Brian's wife and daughter came out; he hadn't seen them since the start of the race so he was really looking forward to it. He had become a grandfather during the race as his son's wife had produced twins, so he was anticipating seeing the photos and hearing baby news. All the boys had girlfriends coming out, so it was really quite exciting.

No-one had been to Cape Town before and I think all of us had preconceived ideas about South Africa. We thought we would immediately notice racial differences and problems but were actually quite surprised to find Cape Town itself more liberal than we had expected. We quickly learned from the locals that Cape

Province has always been fairly open and less enthusiastic about apartheid. Our mooring was at the old dockside called the Victoria and Alfred waterfront where huge developments involving shopping centres, restaurants, bars, hotels and shops had replaced Victorian wharves and warehouses.

Everyone really enjoyed this port. All the crews achieved instant superstar status, being right on show at the front of the dock. The novelty and convenience of having a bar all of twenty seconds walk away was much appreciated. Each of the restaurants in the development had adopted a boat – the first evening we went off to St Elmos, a pizza restaurant, to have our first real food of the past six weeks washed down with real wine and more wine. *Rhone-Poulenc* finished two-and-a-half-hours behind us which gave a further boost to the celebrations. *Heath* finished at 6 o'clock in the morning.

I didn't make it back to my bunk. I fell asleep at the chart table at breakfast time and stayed there until midday; the crew tiptoed past, some taking embarrassing photos. The fleet of ten yachts attracted masses of interest and a continuous stream of visitors who wished to look over them. There was so much friendliness and hospitality that, regrettably, we had to refuse some invitations as there was too little time to enjoy them all.

Coopers Theron du Toit, the South African firm of Coopers & Lybrand were amazingly friendly. They spoiled us with dinners, theatre performances and days out on the sea rescue launch. In return we gave talks and PR interviews which were organised by Pete Smith and Willie Viviers of Coopers. While we were there, they announced that they were changing their name to the international name of Coopers & Lybrand – we teased them about the nautical tradition of it being bad luck to change names.

Wherever you are in Cape Town, Table Mountain stands majestically in view. As a keen walker I was eager to experience the thrill of climbing to the top of this world famous landmark. It was a memorable day – the route we took is not in any guide books, as we had our own guide, Richard, from the local Coopers & Lybrand office, who is a regular climber. The route went along the Kloof Corner ridge which is very impressive, being only sixteen feet wide and with a view looking both north and south when the cloud permitted. I must admit that I felt safer walking on a heaving yacht than on this ridge. I came down the easy way in the cable car but the hard work of the climb was worth it. Some of the more adventurous crew went further afield to Kruger Park, Namibia and up the Garden Route around Cape Province.

One of my proudest moments was when the swiftly recruited *Coopers & Lybrand* running team entered a road relay – a marathon. Matt Steel-Jessop, Brian Bird, David Turner, Mike Bass and Paul Shepherd formed the team, with Paul running in two of the legs. Even with no training for months they managed a creditable time of three hours and thirty-eight minutes, although there were a few sore legs the following day.

Another outing of a rather different sort was arranged by Titch and Richard through the head of security at the waterfront. Two Caspar armed security trucks were used as vehicles for a tour to the black townships. I didn't go, as I really didn't feel it appropriate to go and stare at impoverished people living in very bad conditions. The ten of my crew that did so, however, said that their eyes were opened to the immense immigration from all over South Africa and the surrounding countries – approximately a thousand people poured into Cape Town each day. Housing varied from shacks made out of corrugated tin sheets to two-storey brick houses complete with fenced gardens. Unlike the impression given by media reports in the UK, these areas have developed into complete communities with their own shops, churches and schools as in white suburbia. We found a strong feeling of hope and optimism in South Africa; I don't think they will find an ideal solution but hope that some sort of workable compromise can be found very soon.

Crew changes took place at Cape Town. Mike Bass from British Steel had done the one leg which was planned and Paul Shepherd ('Shep') was joining to take his place. Mike Bass had proved to be brilliant on board. He went through the whole range of emotions from being very nervous at the start (knowing that the rest of us had sailed halfway round the world and he would be the new boy) to being bored with the continual beating and tedium of it all in the middle of the leg. Once he had become more experienced, towards the end, he revelled in the Southern Ocean. He became a thoroughly useful crew member, both on deck sailing and below decks where his practical skills (he was a qualified electrician) were often in demand. We had known Shep as a crew member during the previous year. He has a very broad Yorkshire accent, so when

Shep or Robert were talking on deck no one south of Watford could understand either of them.

Gary, having chosen not to put himself through the seasickness again, was leaving. His replacement was Shane Dixon who was a bank manager from Southampton. Shane was a completely new face and we didn't really know anything about him. He had been involved indirectly with the Challenge since its inception – or had known about it – because he is Chay's bank manager.

On the leg from Hobart to Cape Town it had become apparent to all on board, not just to me, that Titch was not happy in the position as mate, so it came as no surprise when he drew me aside and said he wanted to resign from the job, preferring to enjoy the rest of the trip as a crew member. From my point of view as skipper, this caused an awkward situation. A mate's job is something that all the watch leaders should aspire to – it's like a career structure. If someone decides, for whatever reason, that they don't want to do the job, it casts a shadow over the position. The mate's position ceases to be respected by the crew because the job itself has been devalued. I therefore had to rethink the boat's organisation – the structure of the watches – to avoid appointing a mate on the last leg. I did consider talking to Matt about the mate's position but, at the time, most of the crew were away with friends and it would have been impossible to sound out opinions before the boat was on the move.

In the end, the watch system remained the same with the four watches rolling over at two-hour intervals. The thirteenth person – one watch had four people in it – was always the cooking watch. Every third day, when we changed the timing of the watches and the cooking responsibility from one watch to another, we then moved one person on from one watch to the next. I took over most of the navigation, while the weather information and the routine matters on board, were the responsibility of the watch leaders who were Titch, Robert, Neil and Matt, all equally trusted and respected. Matt's main responsibility was for the boat performance: analysing its course and speed. Neil became more involved with the weather analysis, along with his sail mending capacity. Titch and Richard kept the weatherfax schedules updated and ensured that we pulled in as much information as possible. Robert had the additional responsibility for deck gear as David had taken on the purser/catering role.

Once we'd left the Victoria & Albert waterfront for the re-start, we were slightly horrified to see a huge swell rolling into the harbour entrance. A big wave broke completely over the breakwater with spray 20 to 30 feet high. Having recommended to all our new Cape Town friends that a good place to see the start was actually on the breakwater I was worried that these guests would have been washed off! My assumption was that the start of the race would be quite horrific, with the very large swell rolling and pitching all the yachts but only a gentle 16 knot breeze to drive them.

The wind was just about on the beam to make the turning mark in the bay and we made a clean start in second place, with *Commercial Union* just getting their spinnaker up and slightly pulling away from us; we held on to our No. 1 yankee and staysail combination to go up to the turning mark further up the Bay. The mark was spotted quite soon off starboard, so we were high on the buoy and had to go further downwind – and hence slower – to it, although not far enough downwind to warrant flying the spinnaker. Many of the other boats in the fleet had gone very high. On checking later, we found that the buoy was about a mile further south than the position given in the sailing instructions (although the leg instructions were quite clear in saying it was at this approximate position).

The order of the boats round that mark was *British Steel II* (who had had their genoa up and had started at the very low end of the line), followed by *Commercial Union* and then *Pride of Teesside*, who just pipped us with a call for water at the mark, although we soon got through them on the inside and made third place. The swell was still very, very uncomfortable although nobody was seasick. I'd helmed for the first couple of hours but once past Dassen Island in Table Bay, others began steering. Lack of sailing practice meant we were all a bit rusty and we started losing ground once I'd handed the helm over, but I'm sure this would have been the same on most of the other boats. There were lots of tired people about – the usual syndrome of getting back into the routine. I found it very difficult to sleep as my internal body temperature controls seemed to be completely up the creek, probably due to being overtired as we left port.

That night and during the following day, the wind gradually backed and soon we had the spinnaker up. Our first gybe was a near disaster; the port pole fell into the water, not having its uphaul attached, and our race heavyweight spinnaker – professionally repaired in Cape Town – fell apart for the fourth time an hour-and-a-half after that. Also during the gybe, the downhaul broke on the other pole so the gybe took thirty-five minutes to complete by the time the crew had tidied up all the loose ends. It was very frustrating but it was no use getting upset because such things happen when racing. The crew quickly dropped back into the familiar rhythm of sailing the boat and solving problems very quickly.

Not only were the crew tired but I think the boat herself was a bit tired. The batteries certainly were and for the first two or three days we were having to charge the batteries for about twelve hours a day. The engine was running for five or six hours at a time with only two hours off, as we tried to get a boost charge into the batteries. Although we got used to the noise, it was nice and peaceful when the background droning noise stopped. Our tanks were full of fuel and, if anything, running the engines for power helped to lighten the boat.

The watermaker was also tripping out and making salt instead of fresh water. The boys checked the filters first. The coarse filter on the main salt water inlet was full of slime, small crustaceans (probably krill) and barnacles. Once this was cleared and the two watermaker filters were replaced, it did seem to run a little better. The solenoid switch that changed the valve for either fresh or salt water seemed to have developed an electronic gremlin which would keep switching the system to salt whenever your back was turned! The solenoid switch was controlled by the salinity sensor dial which was turned fully on. Pike and Baldrick investigated and discovered another way to trigger the production of fresh water which involved the 'high tech' application of a small screwdriver between two terminals – as long as it kept going for the next three weeks we weren't too worried about the means.

The main planning aid for plotting our route on this leg came from the US Navy Marine Climatic Atlas. The USN produces charts for all kinds of climatic data and various correlations. They can be viewed or copied at the Met Office library in Bracknell (where I spent many hours the previous summer). The data that has led to these compilations has taken a hundred years or more to assimilate. The most useful charts for race planning, ie trying to find the fastest rather than the shortest routes, have been the isopleths and the sea level pressure charts. The isopleth chart shows lines joining places where the wind speed is less than 10 knots for a particular percentage of time. These charts are produced separately for each month of the year as are the sea level pressure gradient charts. Overlapping these charts it shows the correlation between the data, and the areas with the densest lines should dictate the best route. Areas which showed less than 10 knots of wind for 30 per cent of the time were obviously more favourable than those showing less than 10 knots for 40 per cent of the time. Because the boats sail upwind nearly as well as down, there was no reason for any of the boats to go well west and try to avoid the usual North Atlantic high. I thought it would be obvious to all the skippers that for the extra mileage sailed to be worthwhile they would need a difference between upwind and downwind speed of about 25 per cent. These boats actually perform within about 10 to 15 per cent – the maximum upwind speed is about 9 knots and the maximum downwind speed is about 10.5 to 11 knots. The difference does not warrant sailing a much longer course to go downwind. So we set a slightly curved track on the plotting chart to follow what we generally felt was the windiest route. Until we were well north of the Doldrums, no one would know for sure which route would prove to be best.

Four days out from Cape Town the winds were fairly steady. We were still trying to make the best speed in the best compromise direction and I felt that the yacht was not going quite as well as it should. I was generally very fed up with life. Being very tired didn't help, and if I was off form the whole boat went off and seemed to stop trying. Maybe I was being more critical of what I saw as a very relaxed attitude – too laid back by far. It was 'The Admiral' Martin Wright who opened a conversation about it with a 'wobbly coffee' (laced with Scotch) and pushed me into making up my mind to do something. I think Martin's background and naval training was such that he understood and realised that the skipper's responsibility in a situation like this was very difficult, with a delicate balance to maintain.

He drew me into a crew discussion which enabled me to convey my determination to keep pushing and racing the boat. There was a group on board that agreed with this, but there was no consensus. At this stage I felt that there was little point in dictating tactics because that would cause a division on board. So we set up a watch leader's meeting, followed by a crew meeting. The aim was to go through key statements that had been made by the crew themselves a year ago, at the Chilworth training weekend, on goal setting to see if they still had the same objectives.

The conversation with Martin made me realise that in not having a mate, as such, I had no buffer for making sure that the general routine jobs on board were being done. These included regular writing up of the log, pumping the bilges and making sure the galley was clean. Brian became an executive watch leader, without a watch, to look after these areas of responsibility and was happy to do it. This meant that the watch leaders could concentrate on the sailing; the trim loop was reinstated and new notices were written up to remind people of their boat-speed responsibilities.

The most useful new procedure was to ensure that someone sat at the chart table and fed a ten minute average back up to the deck watch. The ten minute average was based on the course made good over that period of time. This indicated if we were high or low of the track required, the average speed, the best speed if there had been a changeover at the helm, then the new helm's best speed, if the wind direction had changed. So not only were the people on deck sailing, but they had the data feedback at 10 to 15 minute intervals; that proved to be very useful. We had done this on previous legs but had not formalised it to such a degree.

The arrival of the one-leggers revitalised the crew with their fresh, keen enthusiasm. They had undergone some training with us, so integrating them into the team happened virtually overnight, whereas with completely new people like Martin and Shane their initiation into the crew took a lot longer, because we had to get to know them, which took probably all of one leg.

As a completely new crew member, Shane was disadvantaged by not having had the benefit of our training and experience. He was used to running a bank and keeping track of everything that was going on within it. He found it hard to adjust to sticking to just one job, and occasionally drew my wrath and prompted shouts of 'Shane, where are you going?' or 'Shane, man your winch!' He might start off in the cockpit manning a winch then, assuming his job was complete he'd wander off to see if the others needed help on the foredeck. Shane was so keen and enthusiastic that he wanted to be where the action was. I explained the importance of onboard discipline – doing your own job and letting others do theirs. Having Shane as a novice on this leg illustrated to the rest of the crew how much they had learnt and improved in the previous months.

The keys for motivation aboard the boat kept changing and the mood swings altered drastically. The problems were still much the same as those which I had noted on previous legs. This made me think that they were common to every sailing or racing boat, not just specifically *Coopers & Lybrand* or even the Challenge fleet. I had thought, at one point, that the set of problems very much related to the particular structure of the Challenge, but then my views changed. I decided that it was to do with group dynamics and was not necessarily connected to sailing; it could occur in any situation which involved a team.

CHAPTER 14

Return to the North Atlantic

During the second week at sea on the crucial final leg of the race, we were handicapped by a sickness bug that spread through the boat. The first casualty was Arnie who went down on the Monday night with severe sickness and stomach cramps – to the extent that he was obliged to stay in his bunk and miss one watch. At first we thought it may have just been something he'd eaten, but by the time Robert, David and finally 'The Admiral' had gone down with it, the timescale wasn't right for it to be food poisoning – it distinctly seemed like a bug. We initiated a vigorous hygiene campaign, using disinfectant and bilge cleaner twice a day, trying to stop whatever it was spreading any further and causing more problems.

The whole boat became cleaner than it had been since the day we sailed from Southampton. On the Saturday, an entire watch went down: Richard, Matt and Sam – virtually at the same time. They were the last crew members to have severe problems; Neil had been off-colour earlier though not actually sick and one or two of the others had been queasy throughout the week. That only left about four of us 100 per cent fit. The bug only seemed to last 24 hours; after that the victims could return to full duty, although feeling a little bit weak. On average, their appetite took another two days to recover. I think it probably caused us to lose distance since, with this kind of close racing, any minor hiccup costs miles.

By this time we were one of the more easterly boats; two were closer to the African coast and the rest of the fleet was out to the west. The starboard gybe was now becoming more favourable as we were well and truly into the southeast trade winds and they seemed to be swinging more easterly. There was no change foreseen in the weather for the next three or four days. *Group 4* were well to the west and had started moving rapidly again – we prayed their gain would prove shortlived. We very slowly started to take a mile or two from *British Steel II* although both *Heath* and *Interspray* were close on our heels. *Heath* and *Interspray* were the two closest rivals on our overall position at that time so we watched them very carefully. We still tried to get that bit extra out of the boat, all the crew working really well.

By the following Wednesday we'd been sailing for ten days with a spinnaker up, and in the same direction, with much the same winds. Life on board fell into a very familiar pattern; not so much boring, as constant and endless. At the last Chat Show, only 68 miles separated the fleet, from first to tenth place, so the slightest change of wind or swell direction, or boat speed brought intense debate. Why were we losing miles? Our big focus for analysis was not so much where the other yachts were in relation to us at this stage, but at what point they were planning to cross the Doldrums in about ten days time. We knew that the first real break for any of the yachts would come at the Doldrums, so until then it was all a matter of positioning and believing that the spot we were aiming for was the right one to cross. We needed a bit of luck and a lot of prayer. We'd already set the plan for coming up through the trade winds using the route we felt would give the strongest winds. We also had an idea as to where, at that time of year, we felt we should cross the Doldrums – which was a reasonable distance west of the African coast. Until we started getting the information from the Nav Area 2 weather centre out of Toulouse, which gives the Inter Tropical Convergence Zone location, the plan had to remain flexible. Because conditions were likely to change at any time, I needed the resolve to stick to the original plan now that we were in the eastern group. *Heath* and *Interspray* were both within ten miles of us and *Commercial Union* and *British Steel II* were ahead. That at least gave us a target to catch – every mile helped.

From our onboard calculations we found that we had dropped back to tenth position. A bit of a muddle over how long we should have stayed on a particular gybe cost us a few places, but at least it triggered us into looking at the boundary settings of the track built into the plan and deciding how we could stick to it. If you have confidence in a plan it certainly helps to boost people's spirits. If you then change it you must again show complete and utter confidence in the new plan and a good reason for 'binning' the old one. It is important to be flexible and remaining alert and aware of any slight changes in wind direction.

A consensus opinion developed that the starboard gybe was faster. It seemed partly psychological to start with but, when we watched the log and checked it across, there appeared to be a difference of around 0.2 knots. But I remained unconvinced because the 'optimise' function on the GPS showed that the VMG off both gybes was very constant. If I had taken a vote, half the crew would have said that the port gybe was worth a tenth of a knot and half would have said that the starboard gybe was worth the same!

Martin took a lot of teasing around about this time and appeared to take it to heart – being called 'The Admiral' was only the start. Martin had a lot of technical knowledge, but he got his leg pulled because he put it over as a naval officer and the rest of us were not Navy-trained so we hadn't a clue what he was talking about. There was one instance when we saw a ship and 'The Admiral' asked Baldrick what the CPA was. 'CPA? I haven't a clue what the CPA is – what does CPA stand for?' replied Baldrick. It turned out to be the Closest Point of Approach, so Martin spent the next hour explaining to him how to work out intersects on boat courses and speeds and various things like that. He also held forth about how one needed to take a bearing and the only way to take a bearing on a yacht was to actually sight it down the main compass, because any hand-bearing compass on a steel boat was remarkably inaccurate. It became a standing joke, even when he was in earshot: 'There's a ship – what's the CPA then? Oh I'd say about ...'! Martin was a bit surprised about being teased to that extent. He'd been trained to be at sea in a position of authority and now he had to adjust to being a crew member. I think the inter-crew banter affected him more than he expected. It was an indication, however, that he was becoming well and truly baptised as a regular crew member, because you only get full-on teasing from a close group of people.

There were other distractions amongst the crew on this leg. Notably Sam and Arnie became absorbed in playing intensely flirtatious games. Being on the same watch made it far worse. I wasn't sure it was a good idea, especially after we had endured all the stages of Neil and Ann's relationship. It caused a distraction for those on watch with them and disturbed those trying to sleep, because they both become vociferous and noisy when on a high. In the early stages of Neil and Ann's relationship they had become fairly insular and cliquish, but once they became an established couple, everyone was then able to cope with it. I didn't like the idea of having to go through this situation all over again. As it turned out Sam and Arnie just became good friends.

Downwind sailing in the trade winds sounds idyllic, but after the same constant wind and the same sails for six to eight days, the mood actually becomes one of boredom. Any relief coming from a sail change, or torn sail or some deck work was really welcome. There was a lot more wildlife about as we were approximately 200 miles off Ascension Island (still 10° south of the Equator). One day we saw a frigate bird at dawn; later on the same day there was a cry of 'whale' and everyone crowded on deck to look at a sperm whale that seemed to be following the boat. For about five or ten glorious minutes we watched as it either swam alongside or just astern. Suddenly, while we were watching the whale play behind the yacht, we hit something. To our horror we saw a trail of blood behind the boat – a dark pool that spread very quickly. It was obvious that we had hit another whale. Absolute silence fell over the boat; one minute we were really euphoric at seeing these huge friendly mammals swimming with us, the next we felt like murderers. It was really such a sad moment; we were guilty, but we couldn't do anything about it. We just watched helplessly as the trail of blood and guts grew behind us. Thanks to us, the Atlantic Ocean was now minus one sperm whale.

After hitting the whale we checked the top of the keel bolts. Nothing had moved and the yacht appeared to be undamaged. This incident reminded us of the navigation warning that a loose container was floating off the Portuguese coast; it would present a serious problem for the fleet if one of the yachts hit it.

By the 1900 hours Chat Show on April 29 we learned that we'd moved up to ninth place as we had overtaken *Heath*. However, later that night any elation that we may have had in overtaking *Heath* vanished in an instant. Bill Vincent of *Heath* had fallen overboard and they had not, at that time, found him. What dreadful news to have to tell everyone on board. The two watches on deck were immediately told and then each watch was told as they came on duty over the next two hours. The reaction was one of stunned silence followed by the question 'How could it happen now?' After three quarters of the way round the world, for a man to be lost when we were halfway home on the very last leg seemed unbelievable. We sent a message via Coopers & Lybrand in London to advise families, friends and supporters that we were safe, because obviously the news of an incident like this would make people concerned. We sent a message direct to *Heath* on the Inmarsat, basically saying that we were thinking of them all at this time and named all their crew to make the message more personal. That was all we said, just those few heartfelt words.

The mood on board became very quiet – one of sombre sadness. We let feelings and thoughts settle and waited until dawn before we gybed the yacht, when boat awareness had returned. News like that makes you become fairly introspective, trying to analyse how you feel and what you should think. This had been the worst fear for all of us in the Challenge – the skippers, the crew and all Challenge personnel – that we would lose someone; now it had actually happened. At 7 am we took no pleasure in finding ourselves in eighth place. We had overtaken *Interspray* while they had diverted for a while, under instruction, to assist with the search.

The quiet sombre mood continued with sadness and dis-appointment that the Challenge would now lose its good name and record. Everyone was fiercely proud of that record; we had come through 25,000 miles of ocean racing and had very nearly proved that it could be done safely. We tried to understand what had gone wrong. It is human nature to immediately look for reasons, targets for blame. It must have been someone's fault – something must have happened. If you have explanations and reasons it makes the whole event easier to understand. We all wished we could send some comfort over the radio or the Inmarsat to all our friends on *Heath*. They must have felt wretched – a combination of guilt, sadness, anger and shock, and we felt frustrated that we couldn't give them hugs and a lot of confidence.

I truly believe that if Adrian Donovan and the crew of *Heath* were unable to find Bill then no-one else would have been successful. Adrian is a very experienced seaman, coming from the merchant navy. He's been skippering sail training boats and professional charter boats for the last four or five years and he had carried out a lot of safety and man overboard drills as part of his crew training. He had even arranged a special safety weekend in the Solent, throwing crew off the stern, winching them off the boat with helicopters and liferaft practice with all crew in foulies and lifejackets. On *Coopers* I think the news hit Sam the hardest – she became very quiet and obviously very upset. Sam is a 'people person' and she always had the utmost time for all the people within the Challenge. The search was called off at 11.30 BST on Friday with *Heath* rejoining the race.

Discussion on board *Coopers* began to centre around the reporting procedure and contingency plans in the event of a MOB. Robert strongly insisted that a distress message should have been sent straight to a marine co-ordination centre, although we didn't know the true facts of what had happened at the time. From reading the press reports that came through the Challenge, I don't think that as a crew we would have acted differently. We went through a checklist of what we would have done, ie immediate dan buoy launch with a horseshoe lifebuoy, hit the man overboard button on the GPS, rounded up into the wind, got the kite down whether it was whole or in pieces while, at the same time starting the engine. I always insisted on the procedure of launching the small liferaft as a means of finding the MOB or for getting the person back on board if he or she was injured. We would run out the liferaft on 100 yards of floating warp, centre it on the target area and conduct a circular search. I would probably have sent out a MAYDAY call on 2182 Hz, the main calling frequency on the HF set, to alert any vessels close by to assist with the search. *Heath* was in a location that was quite likely to be close to a main shipping route. However, for any ships to be able to assist at that time, they would have had to have been within thirty miles as there were only two hours of daylight left.

On Friday afternoon, the depressed atmosphere on the boat began to lift as everybody began to get involved in plotting and planning for the second 'Crossing the Line' ceremony. On board discussion and artistic talents were being used to the full. Matt and Arnie had a joyful time devising the devilish brew in which to smother the 'criminals'. The indecent relish of some crew members, who were looking forward to the initiation of the new ones, caused some alarm, but it was all in jest, or at least most of it was. We crossed the Equator on May 1 at night, but we postponed Neptune's dues until the cooler part of the late afternoon on the following Sunday. It was an exceptionally hot day; we were slow moving and struggling to make 5 to 6 knots for the first 6 hours and in 12 hours we made just 35 miles. There was some current flowing with us, which must have been the South Equatorial Current but we still needed to maximise boat speed and direction.

As Neptune is renowned for having long hair, there was only one person on board that could fulfil the role – Geraint (Baldrick) Lewis, or Neptune Lewis as he became known. Equator initiates were charged with various heinous crimes; initially of crossing the line without asking permission. Shane's worst crime was that of lending money to Chay Blyth. Shep was accused of both being a Filofax-carrying yuppie and, with his strong Sheffield accent, of bastardising the Queen's English – to which crime he had no choice but to plead guilty. Robert did cross the Equator on the first leg but had got out of the initiation ceremony by virtue of being John Kirk's assistant. On this occasion, he was certainly not going to be allowed to get away with it. His crimes were those of not asking permission to cross the Equator and that he had never started a single leg of this race with a hangover (Robert is teetotal and drinks nothing stronger than chocolate milk). 'The Admiral's' crimes included being at the helm on both occasions when the spinnaker fell apart. We'd also heard that he had related a cheeky tale implying that, on the second leg, it was lucky that he, Martin, knew how to use a sextant on board because he felt that nobody else did! Neptune's regalia consisted of netting and trident plus a cardboard crown covered in tinfoil with strips of blue and green spinnaker cloth as long hair; Bertie made lots of stern, vengeful noises as the foreman of the jury.

Despite the fun, racing was still uppermost in my mind. The tactical question that was exercising me around this time was whether to go inside or outside the Cape Verde Islands. With a thousand miles to go, the weather pattern was anything but stable, making the decision a difficult one. The original plan was to go outside to the west and I still favoured that option. But the northeast trade winds were not due to fill in until 11° north, according to the forecast, and the Inter Tropical Convergence Zone was certainly moving about a lot. The winds were really becoming variable – an indication that we had arrived in the Doldrums. We had our first rain storm, which was just about as drenching as you would imagine a tropical rainstorm to be. We experienced 35 minutes of waterfalls, while just wearing shorts and foulie jackets – everything ran with fresh water. After the initial cooling enjoyment of the first five or ten minutes it actually started getting a little cold.

We still managed to hold our own, position-wise, and it looked as though everyone was aiming to go through the gap to the east between Cape Verdes and the African coast. Having looked at the chart, it would have been an additional 150 miles to go further outside and, with no appreciably better wind or weather pattern out into the Atlantic, it didn't seem likely to pay off. The problem of going outside at that stage was that the prevailing winds would have pushed us further west, increasing the distance still further. I love it when a good plan comes together but, when sailing, you have to be prepared to change it almost at the drop of a hat and let it evolve almost continually. Although plans need to be developed, it's always quite difficult and almost embarrassing to have to explain twelve hours later that the plan has changed yet again.

By the evening Chat Show we found we'd actually gained on everyone in the fleet and were still running in eighth position. The lead regularly swapped between *Group 4*, *Nuclear Electric* and *Commercial Union* but the Doldrums did not split the fleet as might have been envisaged. Instead, the race was even closer, with barely 100 miles separating first and ninth yachts.

We were treated to spectacular sunrises and incredible cloud formations, while at night clear skies stretched endlessly above us. There was no relief from the heat and oppressive humidity, day or night, making sleep nearly impossible. Favourite resting spots were usually in the forepeak on the sail where there was a slight gentle cooling breeze. On one occasion I found four crew there, all snoring in unison. We found very little relief, too, from the burning sun. We used masses of sunblock aided by a variety of hats and T shirts tied in imaginative ways. Only one or two people were badly sunburned, suffering shining, sore noses and tender foreheads.

Cooking in these temperatures was an ordeal for those below in the galley; the chefs would announce that dinner was ready and then escape on deck to drink pints of water to recover. In spite of the conditions we still continued to bake fresh bread because it was so appreciated – everyone developed some talent for it, and we ate a variety of rolls and loaves, both brown and white. Crisp, crunchy coleslaw was another firm favourite but the fresh cabbages cooked slowly in the heat, giving rise to clouds of tiny black flies and a very pungent odour that wafted from their storage boxes.

We finally sailed out of the Doldrums with a resounding send off. The final thunderstorm of this belt of unsettled weather was immense. This climatic tantrum started quickly – the wind increased from 10 to 30 knots and swung 170° from westerly to easterly, catching us totally unawares. It was 5 am, very dark and so impossible to spot the ominous black cloud. With full main and genoa up it was all hands to the foredeck to douse the headsail. Torrential rain was beating down and our work was frequently lit by forks of lightning. It was possible to feel the electrically-charged air, and the rain was very welcome after the oppressive humid heat. With the headsail down and securely lashed to the deck, we went back to the cockpit to sit out the storm. The wind increased to a maximum of 48 knots and, much to my surprise, it continued for nearly two hours; a thrilling time but very hard work at the helm. *Coopers & Lybrand* was joyfully surfing along, with dull boring calms rapidly becoming a distant memory.

When the wind eventually abated to 25 knots we had the chance to check the foredeck and the lashed headsail. Unfortunately, we found that the spinnaker pole had twisted with the force of water and a guardrail stanchion had snapped, leaving two jagged metal edges to cause further damage by neatly shredding our genoa. The head of the sail had broken three hanks and this loose section of sail had been caught and torn by the broken stanchion. Even our experienced *Cooper & Lybrand* sewing circle couldn't manage a repair on this scale.

We were 42 miles behind the lead yacht and in sixth position, working up into the northeast trade winds. We knew we had to sail harder to defray the disadvantage of losing our genoa.

Chapter 15

The End of the Dream

Complete circumnavigation of the world was achieved by *Coopers & Lybrand* when we crossed our outward-bound track on Monday, May 19; our position was 17° 40' north, 19° 56' west, 1255 British Summer Time. This was an indication, as we neared home waters, that our adventure was inevitably coming to an end. It was noticeable aboard that, although we'd achieved this milestone, we didn't actually feel any different now that the magic circle was closed and we had sailed around the world. Did we expect to feel different?

Thoughts aboard the yacht began to turn to the future: where do we go next? What do we do next? Find a job? A career change? These questions were always being asked, in the cockpit and around the saloon table, but very few answers were forthcoming. The easy option was for the few lucky people whose jobs had been kept open; they included David, Brian and Martin. David planned to return to work for the same company as financial adviser on pensions and investments. Brian would be back behind the counter at the shop he owns with his brother, while Martin was to return to being a venture capital investor (another financial man) up in Scotland. However, I think all of us have changed our views. We were certainly not looking forward to having the freedom, clear air and the endless sky taken away.

For the navigator, it was strange to see charts with a good deal more land on them and recognisable shapes like Spain – and there was the south coast of England, creeping into the top right hand corner as we worked our way north. In a way, it was terribly sad. It seemed to be coming to an end so very, very quickly, but there was still a race on. The boats were so close that all the skippers could envisage having a match race back up the Solent.

Because we had been through 95 per cent of the race I was able to give it more thought; the mistakes I'd made, how I would do it differently another time. There is always room for improvement but would it have made any difference? I ended up having a philosophical discussion in my diary and with the other people on board. I was also keen to read more about motivation and team spirit, to see if I had come to the same conclusions as other people. Instead of going on a two-week intensive psychology course, I had taken the hard route and learnt by experience over a year. The experiences had not always been good, but as long as you learn by them and try and find out where mistakes have been made, then hopefully you'll make fewer in the future.

Perhaps in trying to stimulate different people, I should have shouted more loudly or even lost my temper because it would have shown that I was human. I don't think it really does any damage but I wonder if it would have made any positive difference? In the long run it probably wouldn't have done. I still haven't decided whether women leading men presents a problem. I would have to ask a crew member who had sailed under both a male and female skipper. My hunch is that it doesn't make a lot of difference – I had to believe that because if I had started off with doubts about leadership I wouldn't have done this race as a skipper.

My serious mistakes were much more to do with communication with the individuals on board. I've always found that a problem. After a year together I still found it very difficult and was sensitive to criticism, even if I had made a mistake. On the positive side, I had learnt to be a lot more open about the mistakes I made – 'Okay, I made a real pig's ear of that one today, so let's get out of it and do this!'

Initially, at times, I was unsure of myself but felt I had to put on a positive front for the crew's benefit. They needed reliable direction and guidance. Sometimes I had to appear very decisive even when, lacking information, I hadn't made up my own mind about a situation. So I had to use Chay's style – be upfront and say with conviction 'We are going to do this' then, if necessary, tell them 'I've changed my mind, we are going to do that.' Being confident can build confidence, both in yourself and in others.

I was fairly reticent about criticising poor performance because I didn't want to upset people. Whether that's me or whether that's a trait of being female, I don't know. I felt it might be detrimental to the boat and to the crew to upset them. I'd try to point out what I thought was causing a problem and outline what we were going to do about it. It was quite difficult to put over criticism in a manner that was not destructive or accusatory. I was trying to be totally honest, be myself, almost to the raw, rather than treating it merely as a job. I knew the tricks of the trade for remembering things, for motivating people, and I think one thing I have learnt is that, in order to get the most out of yourself and other people, these tricks do actually work. 'Tricks' is the wrong word, they are really skills, little nuances – the art of man-management.

Some of the motivation problems were still exactly the same now as they were on the first leg. Inevitably I wondered whether it was lack of competitiveness on the part of the set of thirteen people that I'd been allocated, or whether I was failing to fire them up in the same way as, say, Richard Tudor? Was it my hand of cards or the way I was playing them?

I think, in the end, it was the way I was playing them. There was nothing wrong with the cards I held. I found it hard to put lessons into practice; I thought that once we'd done a task or manoeuvre once, twice, or three times, then it would become the 'norm'. But it never did seem to become the 'norm', so obviously I didn't work hard enough at keeping a high level of boat awareness. I set standards for myself that are a struggle to reach and then when I've reached them I move on further. That's how I try to motivate myself but not everyone responds to that.

I did learn that when things need doing in a hurry or when some problem occurs, people always do respond. Any major crisis brings out the best in people, whereas routine possibly produces the worst. Generally, the race hasn't destroyed my faith in human nature; I know there's a lot of good in people. No-one who has been involved with the Challenge could regret their involvement at any level. I certainly think it will take a long time for me, and the crew, to appreciate the true scale of what we've actually achieved in the last eight months.

As we neared European waters we encountered the last storm of the race – and it was nothing to do with the weather. A situation arose where one of the boats had requested additional weather information on the North Atlantic High. Another boat had overheard a radio conversation whereby one of the Challenge yachts was receiving, from home, the data position reports from Ceefax (available from any television set) along with the four-hourly reports giving the Course Made Good and Speed Made Good figures. The questions immediately asked by skippers was whether this was within the rules under the clause covering outside assistance?

There had been a lot of discussion about outside assistance prior to the race. The outcome was that we could receive weather information from any public broadcast with the standard equipment we had on board, including weatherfax machines. If we missed a broadcast we could not call up the coast radio station and ask them to repeat it. The suspicion was that maybe someone had been gaining this additional information while the rest of us hadn't. We felt that receiving the position reports from Ceefax – updated four times a day – over and above the positions we were already sent by Race HQ amounted to receiving outside information.

So there were two issues that concerned us: first were we now changing the rules and second, the suspicion that someone had been cheating. Neither were issues that we wanted to even consider as possible, so the airwaves were charged with fairly sensitive discussions between the skippers stating what they had or had not done. Two skippers, who were not present at the Chat Show where this arose, later came on the radio to say that they had not received any outside information on weather and didn't want to be found guilty in their absence from the Chat Show. There was a very strong feeling amongst the skippers that we had all played a fair game and I think that was very true.

The outcome of the row was, from that time on, all yachts were sent the satellite position and speed reports four times a day. It gave skippers additional work in plotting more positions and analysing the figures to see who was doing what. But it also gave us six check times throughout the day to see if anyone had changed their course, or routine, rather than having to wait for a plot every twelve hours, as we had done during the race up until now. We were all absolutely adamant that we had played a fair game so far and it was a shame that this controversy had arisen.

With approximately 12 days to go to the end of the race, the boat was really humming. We were 66 miles behind the lead boats and in sixth place. *British Steel II* had taken the most westerly route and had slowed down, *Hofbrau* was catching up. The worst news, from our point of view was that *Heath* and *Interspray* were also keeping the breeze and taking some miles out of us. On the weather side, with so many faxes and information coming in regarding both the North Atlantic and European waters, both Neil and 'The Admiral' were taking on more of the workload to analyse this data. Everyone was really trying hard and the boat was racing as well as she was able. I felt almost semi-retired when things were going this well.

On Thursday May 13 the high pressure system was filling and there was no wind. Throughout the day, all the boats slowed down – on this particular morning, *British Steel II* slowed more than the others. In light airs we needed to keep trimming to maximise the boat speed and keep the concentration going, sitting to leeward if necessary. We completed 32 miles during that day and it was encouraging that, in the previous ten days looking at the overall figures, we had managed to gain on every boat in the fleet. However, I found the high pressure system a bit of a worry.

We stationed one crewman at the chart table to read out our performance every five minutes, the key figure being waypoint closing velocity. This gave the speed made good in the right direction which then told us which tack was favoured and our fastest point of sail trim. We were acutely aware that our sailing efficiency could not afford to lapse as we had to defray the cost of losing the genoa from our arsenal. With around 1800 miles to go we were lying sixth and only 62 miles behind *Group 4*, the leading yacht. We had only 4 knots of true breeze so we put weight back on the leeward side and eased out the sails. If we had carried any horses on board they would certainly have gone over the side, as ships in previous centuries used to do to lighten their load in this area, known as the Horse Latitudes. As an indication of how seriously we were racing on this leg, we ditched the food stocks to get rid of surplus weight. With seventeen days to go, all the menus were reallocated and each day's food was put in one of the red storage boxes. Anything biodegradable that wasn't required was thrown over the side and any food left over at the end of each day was also jettisoned. Throughout the voyage we kept a strict discipline of compacting and storing any plastic refuse items and disposing of them in port.

It only takes three or four hours without wind and with the boat scarcely moving to change the whole mood on board. The crew became quiet and morose in the belief that the race was finished and over with, but it was not over, not by a long, long way. The sea at times was completely mirror like with only a few gusts or wriggly bits on the surface – the wind changing by 100° swings. We made lots of sail changes in attempts to find a combination and stay on track. This 'parking lot' was at a very similar latitude to the one in our first leg, bringing back bad memories. I reminded the crew, by drawing diagrams, of how far the apparent wind comes forward of the true wind when you are moving in only 3 or 4 knots of breeze. It's very difficult to maintain the boat on a steady course without being pulled into the apparent wind and stalling the boat completely, especially on these steel boats which are so very heavy and slow to respond. As an indication of how easy it was to go nowhere in a hurry in these circumstances, we actually sailed past the same elastic bands that had come off the lightweight spinnaker on a hoist an hour and twenty minutes earlier.

Sunday May 16 saw a change in the weather. Immediately spirits and moods picked up on board: what an improvement it was! Even my mood rose quickly. It was a cracking day averaging 10 knots of boat speed until disaster struck – the promotional spinnaker blew. The kite unzipped right across the main logo in the centre of the sail, severing the 'Coopers & Lybrand' partnership. We then had two key sails down below beyond repair. What really impressed me was that the crew had the asymmetric spinnaker up and drawing in about four minutes. It had happened at a watch change and I missed most of it, being asleep; it was only the halyards running on the hoist that woke me up. I thought 'What a great crew!' It was an indication of how experienced our crew had become.

It was interesting to see a book that had been a favourite on the first leg (virtually as an instructional manual), *One Watch At A Time*, now being reread avidly by everyone on board. It was an account of Skip Novak's voyage aboard *Drum* in the Whitbread Race eight years ago. This time it was being scrutinised in the light of the crew's own experience. They inspected all the photos very carefully. There is one photograph that shows the great joy and excitement and thrill of surfing aboard *Drum* and hitting the top speeds, although their log only shows 15 knots and here we were touching 14 to 15 knots on surges. The crew had expected that the maxis and lightweight boats would go much quicker than our steel 'cruising' boats. I felt that this crew could certainly hold their own with sailors anywhere in the world.

The wind had increased and it had become excellent reaching weather with the asymmetric kite up. If you missed a wave then you needed full lock on the wheel to bring it back on course. The attitude to the asymmetric spinnaker now was almost one of a favourite sail – what a change from four months ago. It was still very difficult to use and it was hard work to maintain the balance between being too far off the wind and too high. With the tendency of the asymmetric kite to broach the yacht, we still needed to have our most sensitive drivers at the helm during these conditions. However, the boat was really tanking along doing 9.5 or 10 knots on a fetch.

We started to feel close to home especially when we picked up Radio 4 and *The Archers* for the first time. Robert and I sat listening to the Shipping Forecast, truly a sign of being in home waters. Another indication was that there was a lot more shipping about and commercial traffic.

If our crew were weary after 28,000 miles, so were the sails. The main was tired and very stretched, but with a thousand miles to go there could be no let up. All our hearts were firmly fixed on fourth place overall and, if possible, a fourth place again on this leg if not better. The crew were working hard and didn't want to let go. We knew we had made mistakes but generally we felt we had also had a touch more bad luck than others – for example 24 hours in that flat spot rather than the 12 hours the other yachts spent becalmed. We fell back from being within 20 miles of *Commercial Union* to 87 miles behind. Still that's sailing and it can happen to anyone.

It was 5 pm and I was helming when Arnie said, 'There's something over there'. About 100 yards off the port beam was the wrecked hull of a dismasted catamaran. It was about 50 feet long, bright yellow and called *Zeeman*. We tacked to enable us to go and have a look and stand by. We sent a telex message via Race HQ to MRRC at Falmouth to enquire about the vessel. The incident created huge excitement on board; there were suggestions of salvage and all sorts of wild speculations about what had happened and whether there might be anyone alive. I had a feeling that the boat had been drifting around for quite a while because, although it was still floating, it was badly damaged. We made a lot of noise on two or three passes but there was no sign of any movement or sound on board. We waited 20 minutes and received a message that the Falmouth rescue centre knew all about it. The singlehanded sailor on *Zeeman* had been picked up injured and taken to Madeira after he'd hit a container. We then set *Coopers* back on course; the encounter had cost us about 45 minutes and with the tightness of the racing, we would have to request a redress of the same amount of time. The delay could cause us to lose a whole position on this leg.

Two days away from the finish, time seemed to pass more slowly as we approached Southampton. We felt we wanted to stay awake longer, not always sleeping when off watch, certainly not during the day. Perhaps it was natural for us to want to get back to a 16 hour day and 8 hour night rather than 4 hour watches. We had sailed about 28,000 miles and had only 400 to go. The distance looked so small on the world chart on the saloon bulkhead.

Everyone ashore wanted constant updates on our estimated time of arrival. It was not easy to give a fixed time since sailing does not run to a set timetable or an organised finish. We couldn't afford to worry about it. For the shoreside team, however, it was a nightmare, especially with the fleet arriving during a weekend or just after. The mood aboard was relaxed yet excited at being so close to the finish and to other yachts. We expected to have a match-racing duel up the Solent, probably with *Hofbrau*. It looked as though we would be fourth overall as *Interspray* was 100 miles behind. Even with any allowance they had been given, *Heath* were still 500 miles behind us and just missing the weather systems. It seemed so unfair, especially with what they had been going through.

On Saturday morning, with a day to go, *Hofbrau* was spotted behind us. We headed up a bit with the asymmetric spinnaker to keep the speed up and chose to go inside the island of Ushant. However, the wind then was heading us and we ended up going outside the island but on the inshore passage. *Hofbrau* diverged to go further west down the main northbound shipping lane where there were many ships passing in and out of the English Channel. It looked as though the race was going to end up being a beat up the Channel against spring tides – the comment back from the crew was 'super'. 'Super' had become an 'in' word in response to anything relating to course and speed. A beat against the spring tides would, however, knock our ETA on the head – maybe I should have stuck to saying Monday morning instead of Sunday evening.

We were getting regular updates and saw *Hofbrau* four miles behind us. Then, during the day, they dropped back to about eight or ten miles behind us as we were further east. Through Saturday night we tacked in the wrong place – south of Start Point. Pete Goss on *Hofbrau* got that one right, but then, as a Plymouth boy, these are his home waters. The following morning *Hofbrau* was ahead of us by one or two miles. Halfway across Lyme Bay at dawn, there they were – leading to leeward. They had their genoa up and we cursed because ours was out of action; it was essential for these light winds. There was no possibility of repairing it, however hard we tried. Parts of it had been ripped into strips 4 inches wide and 16 feet long. The leech had been torn completely off over half the length of the sail.

I'd spent two hours, early in the morning, planning the tides in the Channel and the Solent. We still had some tide with us coming up to Portland and as long as this wind held, although only 10 to 12 knots true, then we would get past Portland Bill before the tide turned. *Hofbrau* was pointing higher than us, and going a touch faster. We maintained our speed by sailing a degree or two freer. Getting closer to Portland the wind headed us and neither of us was going to make it past the Bill. *Coopers* went very close into the western side of Portland and tacked at the last possible moment when we knew we were losing the tide. *Hofbrau* then tacked inside us so we were both heading southeast. At that point, when clear of Portland, *Hofbrau* tacked back northeast and carried on in towards the eastern side of Portland and high into Weymouth Bay. We carried on, partly because the tack was very nearly favourable with the tide still with us. The last wind header had cost us 20 minutes and it meant that the tide was more favourable going east for longer, slightly further south, so we stayed on that tack. By the time *Hofbrau* realised this, and tacked out to follow us, they were a mile-and-a-half astern.

So there we were, with a real battle set up and 30 miles to go to the Needles. They still had the edge on us with speed because we were lacking our genoa; they were slowly catching us. The wind held for at least two or three hours making 120° a good course – and then we were headed. I favoured coming north and probably close-tacking along the shore up to Anvil Point rather

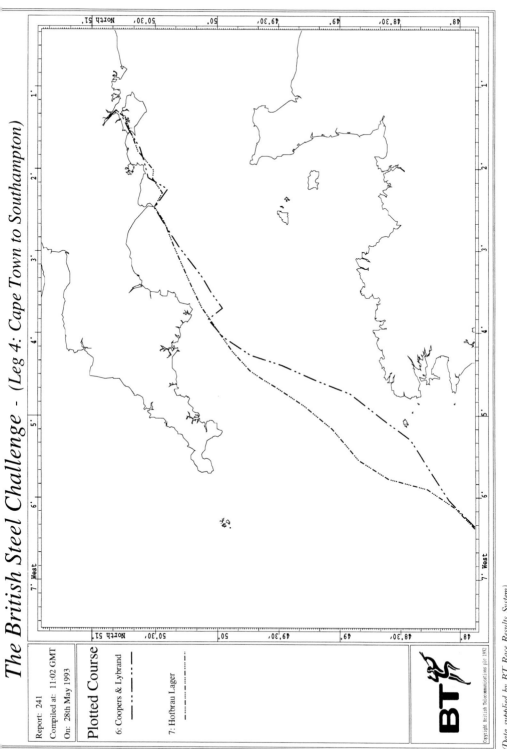

The British Steel Challenge - *(Leg 4: Cape Town to Southampton)*

Report: 241
Compiled at: 11:02 GMT
On: 28th May 1993

Plotted Course

6: Coopers & Lybrand

7: Hofbräu Lager

(Data supplied by BT Race Results System)

than staying offshore, although we'd suffered a bit getting there. *Hofbrau* tacked with us, came up and then tacked to go southeast again. There was a lot of excitement – 'They've tacked, they've tacked, we've got to cover them, we've got to follow them!' So we tacked back and found that we were making a course of about 150° which was not in the direction I wanted to go and we weren't even making any miles in that right distance. So, instead of continuing to cover them we tacked back north and short-tacked the boat between St Albans Head and Anvil Point. Everyone was on deck, winching, steering and working furiously. We had forgotten how difficult it was to short-tack this boat up a coastline and we were tacking within 50 yards of the rocks off St Albans Head.

That tactic did actually give us, I think, four miles on *Hofbrau* but again they still had the better speed (and the genoa); by the time we made the Needles we had a bare mile and a half on them. What a way to complete a round the world race! You couldn't have scripted anything better. The crew had worked superbly with little sleep, and I'd certainly been awake for over 24 hours. Race fever had finally well and truly gripped everyone. We were constantly looking behind, watching *Hofbrau* – so determined to beat her in. It was wonderful. There was an atmosphere of almost bewilderment on board when we saw the first spectator launch coming to greet us out at the Needles. It was then 7.30 pm; they'd been waiting for a long time and were delighted to see us in. As we came further up the Solent, more and more boats gathered around *Coopers & Lybrand*.

The noise level that hit us as we neared the finish line was incredible – a cacophony of boat hooters and cheering spectators. Suddenly I saw a Cunard Line ship going out with a ferry following it; I couldn't see the flashing green lights on the buoy because the crew were standing in front of me; then one of the motor launches in front put a huge, dazzling spotlight on us – I couldn't see a thing. It was chaos! The whole atmosphere was euphoric and I thought 'If I hit something now, tough luck!' I couldn't see the water ahead of me anyway, so I should relax and just enjoy it!

We listened for the update coming from the boys heroically stuck down below at the chart table. A mile and a half to go to the finish; the fairway buoy was just off to the starboard side, getting closer, getting closer – 0.7 of a mile to go to the finish line – Wow! We were there! We'd done it! Just at that moment I think everyone was stunned. We simply carried on sailing; no-one wanted to lose that magic moment. The noise was overwhelming: foghorns – guns – shouts – screams. It was 10 pm and at the Town Quay there were crowds of people waiting. Rod Perry and Brandon Gough came aboard with a case of champagne to celebrate whilst the crew dropped the sails, and cleared the deck in absolutely record time, then we were ready to go in.

The fact that *Hofbrau* was a mere nine minutes behind us was rivetting. Coming out on top in a duel like that, after it had been such a nail-biting race over the last day and a half, was exhilarating enough, but to race round the world to finish nine minutes apart – that was unbelievable.

We motored round into the marina and, again, the first thing that hit us was the noise, with a band playing at full blast. Then, with a shock, we were aware of thousands of people. In the marina people crowded the decks of all the yachts and motor boats and filled every vantage point on the quayside. We revelled in the sheer volume of applause and cheers. It looked as though the pontoon was actually sinking with the weight of well-wishers. Distracted, I thought 'How does a girl park a boat in these circumstances?' I pointed it in the general direction and prayed that the boat would end up in the right place. Suddenly we were in and the boat was swamped with people and champagne. Chay was one of the first on board with congratulations, urging us to wave to the crowd. Neil had mentioned that there would be a few of his family and people from his local pub to greet him but almost at once we became aware of a whole boatful shouting, 'We want Neil! We want Neil!' and he just couldn't believe it. His local pub, the *Five Bells* in Salisbury, had chartered a motor boat to come out and welcome him home.

I think I finally arrived at my hotel at about 3 am. Although I hadn't slept in over a day, I was so excited and hyped up that I didn't want it to stop.

Back in Southampton, the eight months at sea seemed like two days. I'd never had a finish line like that before, it was an emotional experience. The crew were overwhelmed. Never in their wildest dreams did they think that the finish would make such an impression on them, or would attract such a huge number of people. We found it quite awesome.

Eight boats finished in seventeen hours – one after another –

and it must have been quite a day for the spectators that had been patiently waiting. The finish could scarcely have been planned better – on a fine Sunday with six of the boats finishing in daylight with billowing spinnakers. I loved our night time finish with the lights reflecting on the water; it was very atmospheric. Above all, I was delighted to hear that John Chittenden and *Nuclear Electric* had won; the experience and superb seamanship of this wily old man of the sea had prevailed. All credit to him and his crew.

The final words

The last two yachts came in during the next three days and received a rousing welcome home as the final members of the Challenge family. This was probably to be the last time that the whole Challenge fleet would be seen on the water together. Our feelings were not altogether those of sadness – more a sense of rock solid relief at a satisfactory ending to a huge adventure, marred only by the tragic loss of Bill Vincent. Everyone had completed what they had set out to achieve more than four years ago. The true scale and importance of that achievement will only dawn on us all in the months or even years to come.

Appendices

Challenge
Yacht Specifications

Rig	Bermudan cutter rig	
LOA	67 ft	20.42 m
LWL	55 ft	17.76 m
Beam	17 ft 3 in	5.26 m
Draught	9 ft 3 in	2.82 m
Top of mast from waterline	85 ft 3 in	25.98 m
Height of mast above deck	79 ft 5 in	24.20 m
Displacement	33 tons	
Ballast keel	12 tons	
Sail area		
inc 100% foretriangle	1932 sq ft	179.49 sq m
Main	926 sq ft	86.02 sq m
Genoa	1480 sq ft	137.49 sq m
Spinnaker	3780 sq ft	351.17 sq m

Accommodation:	
Berths	14 (6 cabins)
Saloon	1
Galley	1
Heads	2
Drying/oilskin room	1
Chartroom/deckhouse	1

Engine:	
Type	Mermaid Ford 6 cylinder naturally aspirated diesel
HP	120
Generation	2 x 100 amp hour alternators (battery capacity 800 amp hours)
Electrics	24 volt

Watermaker	Aquafresh 800ED
Fuel	418 gal 1900 lt
Water	242 gal 1100 lt
Instruments	Autohelm ST-50 series
GPS	Magnavox
SSB radio	Skanti 8400S
VHF	Skanti 3000
Radar	Raytheon R20x
Mast	Proctor Masts
Sails	Hood
Winches/deckgear	Lewmar
Standing rigging	Norseman Gibb Dyform
Running rigging	Marina

Construction:

Hull	50B mild steel
Deck	316 stainless steel
Designer	David Thomas
Working drawings	Thanos Condylis
	(C & S Yacht Designs)
Builder	Devonport Management Ltd
Project Manager	Andrew Roberts

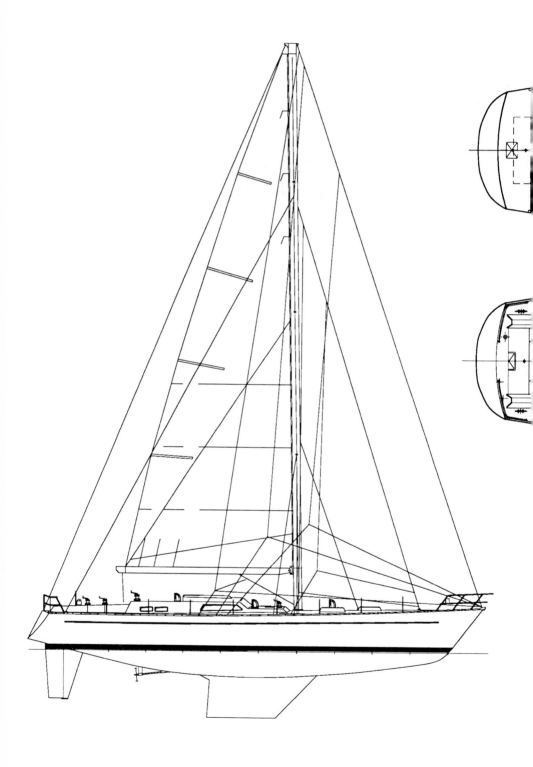

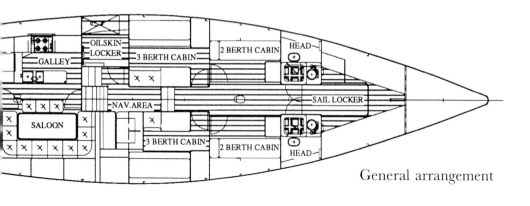

General arrangement

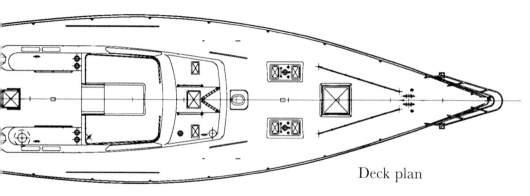

Deck plan

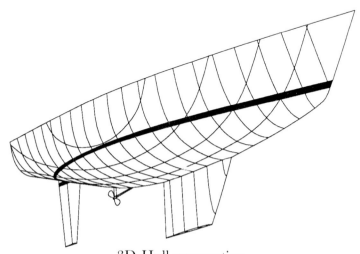

3D Hull perspective

APPENDIX 2

Coopers & Lybrand Crew

Legs 1–4

Vivien Cherry, 33, skipper, Engineering services manager, Wokingham
Brian Bird, 51, Butcher's shop owner, Plymouth
Robert Faulds (*'Fraser'*), 29, Printing shop manager, Glasgow
Richard Griffith (*'Bertie'*), 49, Director, London
Geraint Lewis (*'Baldrick'*), 30, Computer systems designer, Teddington
Maarten Malmberg (*'Arnie'*), 23, Student, Rotterdam
Neil Skinner (*'Hodges'*), 34, HGV driver, Wiltshire
Matthew Steel-Jessop (*'Pikey'*), 29, Computer network manager, London
Paul Titchener (*'Titch'*), 29, Management consultant, London
David Turner, 33, Financial consultant, London
Samantha Wood, 23, Student, Stafford

Leg 1: Southampton to Rio de Janeiro

Ann de Boer (*'Cloggy'*), 26, Public relations consultant, Netherlands
Murray Findley (*'Godfrey'*), 61, President-Sobel Linen, Las Vegas
John Kirk (*'Jonesey'*), 49, Outdoor activities instructor, Bideford

Leg 2: Rio de Janeiro to Hobart

Ann de Boer
Phil Jones, 28, Steel worker, Port Talbot
John Kirk

Leg 3: Hobart to Cape Town

Mike Bass, 28, Engineer, Stoke on Trent
Gary Hopkins, 35, Local government manager, Chigwell
Martin Wright (*'The Admiral'*), 34, Investment manager, Glasgow

Leg 4: Cape Town to Southampton

Shane Dickson, 44, Bank manager, Southampton
Paul Shepherd ('*Shep*'), 39, Fitter and trade union official, Sheffield
Martin Wright